What's Under a Rock?

by ROBERT GANNON

illustrated by Stefan Martin

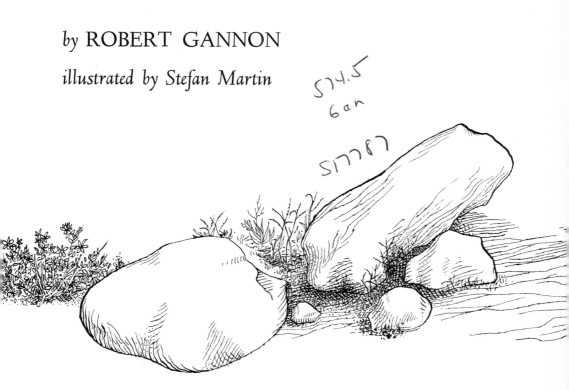

E. P. DUTTON & CO., INC. NEW YORK

Published simultaneously in Canada by Clarke,
Irwin & Company Limited, Toronto and Vancouver

SBN: 0-525-42475-x
Library of Congress Catalog Card Number: 71-133114

Designed by Hilda Scott
Printed in the U.S.A.
Second Printing, February 1973

To
Mark Kossuth, age 13,
my teacher, for his
patience in the face
of slow-wittedness

Acknowledgments

Help. When you write a book you need it. And I culled aid from any number of people. Here are a few:

Tom Carroll, biologist with the Rondout Valley (N.Y.) School System

Walter Ebeling, Professor of Entomology, University of California, Los Angeles

Thomas Eisner, Professor of Entomology, Cornell University

David Krieg, Assistant Professor of Biology, State University College, New Paltz, N.Y.

H. F. Loomis, diplopodologist with the Agricultural Research Service, United States Department of Agriculture, Miami

Marcia Newman, freelance micro-paleobotanist

John Novi, owner of Depuy Canal House Tavern in High Falls, N.Y. (in whose attic room the book was written)

Le Roy B. Nydegger, Professor of Biology, State University College, New Paltz, N.Y.

Richard J. Ordway, Professor of Geology, State University College, New Paltz, N.Y.

Helen E. Osburg, Assistant Professor of Microbiology, State University College, New Paltz, N.Y.

Robert W. Pyle, President of John Burroughs Natural History Society and Professor of Biology, State University College, New Paltz, N.Y.

Daniel Smiley, ecologist and former governor of The Nature Conservancy

Alfred V. Zamm, allergist, Kingston, N.Y.

. . . and these professional writers who checked me out on clarity: Blanche Schiffman, James R. Berry, Hans Fantel, Ken Gilmore, Dennis O'Neil, and Tad Richards.

Grateful acknowledgment for permission to quote copyrighted material is given to the following:

Houghton Mifflin Company, *Ways of the Ant,* John Crompton (1954)

Peter Farb, *Living Earth,* Harper & Row (1959)

McGraw-Hill Book Company, *Fieldbook of Natural History,* E. Laurence Palmer (1949)

Cornell University Press, *Handbook of Nature-Study,* Anna Botsford Comstock (1911, 1939, 1957)

Tillson, N.Y.   ROBERT GANNON
Spring, 1971

Contents

What's Under a Rock?

1. The Rock

Tip up a rock—almost any that has been resting for a time in the woods, in a park, in a meadow. Sometimes the ground is alive with movement: ants rushing to carry off their larvae; pill bugs, like tiny, armored tanks rumbling blindly to another war; sleepy salamanders grumbling and plodding to the nearest darkness; 1/16-inch spring-tails, now here, now with a tail spring, vanished.

Lift another rock and the world it covers seems deserted. You can't see a wiggle. But life is there, nonetheless. Wait a minute, be patient, and you'll note a movement here—a bit of fungus turns into a worm. There, a seed case jiggles; it's a pupa. Now a root tip bends, pulling itself down a hole. An earthworm.

A tiny seed looks a little too bright. You nudge it with a straw and it scurries off on little beetle legs, slipping and stumbling and falling in panic among the beetle-size boulders, before frantically diving headfirst down a crevice.

Odd, but when you've been lying for fifteen minutes, magnifying lens in hand, peering at the miniature empire in the dent made by the rock, the outside world—your world—suddenly seems remote and unreal. Instead of feeling yourself a giant, you shrink to the size of the world you're watching. And when a monster centipede trains toward you, automatically you want to hide behind a clump of soil.

This miniature world hidden by a boulder contains a fantastic variety of insects, plants, worms, and bugs living together in a tiny, nearly self-contained environment. The system is a *cryptosphere*, which means "hidden world," and which refers to that space a few inches below the surface of the earth protected by leaves, humus, mosses, and stones. Its inhabitants are *cryptozoa*.

The quantity of life beneath a rock is enormous. The population of a square foot of ground—most of them microscopic—can number more than the human inhabitants of the entire planet.

Some of the cryptozoa are born here, mature, reproduce, and die without ever seeing the sun. Many have eyes so primitive they can tell only if the world is light or dark. Other creatures hide in the cryptosphere by day, then emerge at night when the sun's hot and drying rays are gone. Still others spend *most* of their existence under the rock, then near the end of their lifetimes emerge for only an hour or two—time enough to mate, find a suitable place to start a new colony, and die. And then some that are born here move away early in their life cycle, shunning the darkness of the rock's underside. In *their* closing hours of life they must spend at least a few moments under the rock laying eggs.

The miniature world under a rock in Mississippi is not exactly the same as one in Idaho. A rock-world in the New Jersey Pine Barrens is not the same as one perched atop Mount Washington in New Hampshire. In fact, no two rocks—even those next to each other—hide identical *eco-systems* (which is another term for closed universes).

But all rocks have certain things in common, and one that is "typical," that can be used as an example of what you may see under a slab of stone in the backyard or nearby woods or city park, isn't too hard to find.

Such a typical rock is the one this book is about. It happens to be in New York State, ninety-seven miles north of New York City. It's on my farm, about a half mile from the house. I've been watching it for about five years now, and I think I know it—and the world it hides—pretty well.

The rock is as big around as a garbage-can cover. It rests forty feet up the side of an open woodland hill, facing south, sticking out of the decomposing leaves and brown earth. It forms a small ledge. Around it are oaks, maples, and a few elms dying of Dutch elm disease.

The rock wasn't always perched on the hill, of course. It didn't come from anywhere around there, in fact, but from a couple of hundred miles north, near what is now called Lake Placid. It originally was part of a mountaintop in the Adirondacks, thrusting itself thousands of feet above the surrounding valleys. But nearly twenty thousand years ago the mountain was buried under a glacier, under snow so squeezed it had become solid ice.

Fed by winter-long snowfalls, the ice mass slowly moved south like white tar. It carried rocks, boulders, and even whole small hills along with it. The rock was ripped from its birthplace by another boulder pressed against it, and it lodged in nearly the center of the floe. Years later, when the ice finally melted, the rock was dropped very near the place where it rests today.

Each summer, as the years passed, earthworms working around the rock tended to bury it, and each winter

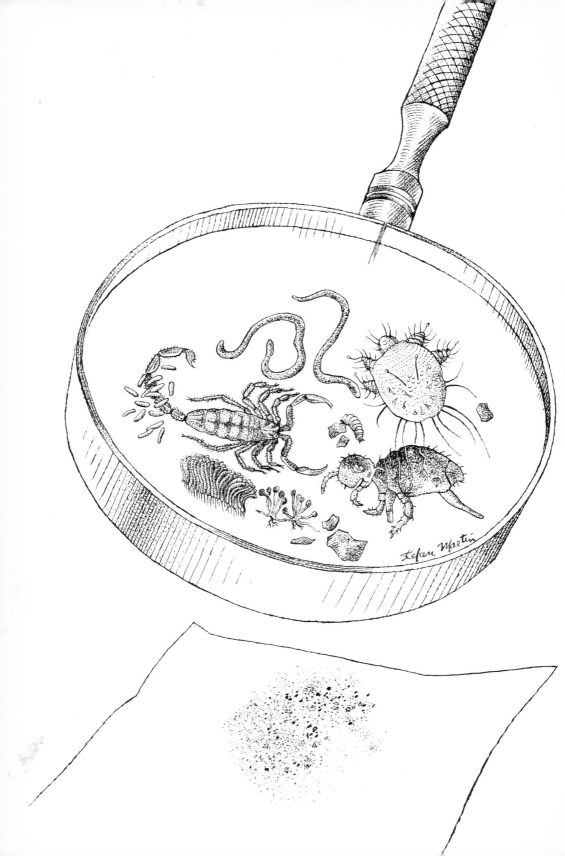

2. In the Soil

The earth itself, under and around the rock, is boiling with life. Trouble is, no one can see most of it without a microscope.

Take a spoonful of soil and sprinkle it on a large piece of white paper or old bedsheet and what do you see? Usually, not a thing. At least not right away.

But wait a moment. You may notice a tiny gray-black speck or hair-tip walking energetically in erratic circles. The drunken bug is probably a springtail, a *collembolan*. Move toward it and if it *is* a springtail it'll vanish—to reappear more than a foot away.

The mechanism for this fantastic jump is a forked, kangaroolike tail spring attached to the rear of the animal. It's stretched forward toward the abdomen and held taut underneath with tiny hooks. When the springtail wants a fast getaway, he releases the hooks and the spring snaps him backwards eighteen inches or more—the equivalent of a person being hurled two city blocks. Often as not he lands on his back. But he scrambles to his feet again,

From top right, moving clockwise: mite, springtail, fungi, pseudoscorpion, roundworms.

9

quickly tucks his tail into the cocked position, and gets set for another trip.

Springtails are insects, but they have no wings and undergo no metamorphic change (from *larva* to *pupa,* then adult) as do most other insects. Instead, the six-legged adult looks as though it never passed the larval stage.

Most entomologists believe that except for the tail spring, springtails are very much like all insects were at one time. In fact, they probably are direct descendants of insects that lived 300 million years ago. Somehow evolution passed them by.

Some springtails are long and thin (though none are longer than 1/5 inch), while others are hunched over so that they seem globular. These are about the size of the period at the end of this sentence. When you first trap one of the hunched kind under a magnifying lens you'll probably smile, for somehow the things look comical, like a child's drawing of a bug.

Springtails that live on the surface of the earth—next to the face of the rock or hidden among the leaves or even dancing on the snow—are pigmented brown, blue, light-yellow. Others live in the earth itself. Spending all their time underground, they have no need for sight, so they lack eyes; nor for protective coloration, so they are color-lessly milky. They live on decaying plant bits and fungus spores, plus waste matter of other creatures, covered with nourishing bacteria. In turn, springtails rank high on the diet of many other crypto-creatures, and so are vital to the ecology, the balance, of the under-rock world.

Altogether, estimates one expert, two thousand different springtail species are leaping about. A few years ago a researcher in New York State carefully counted the number of individual springtails and other creatures in a square foot of earth one inch deep. Among the 1,356 animals were 265 springtails. Some soils contain ten times that amount.

In the same count the researcher found four times as many mites as springtails, and some searchers have counted nearly twenty times as many in other soil.

Mites are *arachnids,* not insects. They have eight legs (like spiders), not six (like springtails), sticking out of beanlike bodies. Also, insects have three body segments— head, thorax, abdomen—where arachnids have only two. The head and thorax are combined. And arachnids, unlike insects, have no antennae.

Mites are tiny, so small you can't see most of them unless you check with a magnifying glass. And because the majority live underground (the *oribatid* group), and have pretty dull lives, entomologists have spent little time studying them.

A few mites, however, have been looked at closely, and their lives make curious reading. One, for example, is the spruce-needle mite. It calls the needle home for the first half of its life, then moves out into the world.

First, the fallen spruce needle is attacked by fungi, ever present in the forest soil. Then the tiny mite moves in to live on the soft, mealy inside—one mite to one needle. At just about the time the inside is all eaten, the mite is an adult.

Another highly studied mite—examined mainly because it affects man—is the chigger or harvest mite. This rust-colored, rather fuzzy fellow—called red bug in parts of the South—is closely related to the red spider mite which at-

tacks house plants. He spends most of his life underground, out of harm's way, a bother to no man. But the
brief period of his existence above ground makes up in
nastiness for all the subsurface peace.

When the chigger egg hatches in the summer months,
the tiny larva—smaller than the eye can see—lives for a
time on littler mites and other bits of living stuff found in
the soil. Then it craves mammal flesh. So on a warm, moist
day (a chigger can't stand much dryness), it wriggles to
the surface, then crawls up a blade of grass or a bush until
it can climb no higher. If, along the way, it bumps into one
of its fellows, it stops, and the two of them sit there.
Others may come along, touch, and stop, until a hundred
or more chiggers are gathered in one spot, waiting.

They're looking for some animal to come along. When a
shadow passes over the bunch, everybody stands up and
starts waving, hoping to snag a ride. Tiny hooks on their
legs are efficient. A brush, and they've caught onto a passing animal.

If the animal is a man, the chigger scurries through the
weave in his clothing. It nestles in a place where the material binds—under the belt is a favorite—there to spend up
to a week, head buried in skin, eating. It injects a peculiar
kind of saliva which liquefies portions of the host's tissue.
Then the mite sucks this predigested meal into its body.

When gorged, it drops onto the soil. The host continues
to itch for four or five days. If the earth is warm and light
and moist, the mite digs downward, to live a few more
days as a larva. Then it molts into an adult, and stays in the
cryptosphere for the rest of its life.

Mites perform an extremely important function in the
ecology of the soil. Along with other minute animals, most
mites live on decaying plant matter. They break it into

smaller pieces, digest it, then redeposit it. Then the material is attacked by bacteria and converted to its base chemicals, which plants absorb, to complete the cycle.

Without mites and other such organisms, the matter would eventually break down, but the process would be much slower. Other mites keep the underground world in balance by living on the eggs of spiders, insects, and fellow mites.

Generally, mites are relatively safe from their enemies. Three reasons for this: First, many of them have tiny legs that whip up close to their bodies at the first alarm. Enemies often pass them by, unnoticed. Second, they've got tough bodies. A predator may try a sample, but the armor often is too strong to break. And third, to some predators mites taste terrible. "Often they are rejected after a single touch," reported one old naturalist. "A spider which bites a mite will not infrequently retire to wipe its mouth on the ground."

Another fascinating little crypto-creature is the *pseudoscorpion,* or false scorpion, also an arachnid. It's usually about 1/8 inch long, is equipped with a pair of formidable pincers, and looks like a miniature lobster or scorpion without the tail. The tiny animal also has a couple of smaller pincers alongside its mouth, the better to hold and tear apart its prey. It devours springtails, mites, and other cryptozoa in great quantities, and helps keep those populations in some sort of balance.

Pseudoscorpions spin nests of silk, then fill them with eggs. The female tucks the nests against her belly, where they stay until the young hatch. They remain stuck there a few days more—feeding, meanwhile, on a milky substance —scorpion milk—secreted by the mother.

Sometimes you see false scorpions grasping the legs of daddy-longlegs, hitching a ride, to move long distances without expending much energy.

The frontier between the visible and invisible creatures living under the rock is one millimeter—about 1/25 inch; anything smaller can't be seen clearly by the human eye. One creature that straddles this border is the *nematode,* or eelworm, which averages just about a millimeter long.

Nematodes are roundworms that look like slender eels without the segments that earthworms have. Often they seem like thrashing smidges of hair or thread. In fact, nematode means threadlike.

Some nematodes are gigantic. The human hookworm, for instance, grows to a yard or more. But most of the worms likely to be found living under the rock are a millimeter or less, smaller than one-third the size of the dot on this "i."

Nematodes are engrossing creatures, and because they cause an enormous amount of damage to crops, scientists have studied them enough to know most of the details of their private lives. One type lives in the boiling waters of hot springs, while others thrive in the icewater of thawing Antarctic ice floes. Some live in the gullets of fish. Others inhabit man's appendix, and apparently can live nowhere else. One species lays only a few eggs a day, while another produces two hundred thousand. Still others lay no eggs at all; they bear their young alive.

The tiny nematodes can be tough. Some of them can go into a dormant stage and remain in suspension indefinitely. One group of botanists found nematodes alive and well in kernels of wheat sealed for twenty years.

This suspension stage is brought about by some nematodes who deposit eggs inside their own bodies. The adult fills itself with eggs like a stuffed sausage, until almost the whole body contains eggs and nothing else. Then, quietly, it dies. The tough, leathery cuticle then becomes a protective shield that can withstand boiling water, subfreezing temperatures, floods and droughts, caustic chemicals.

But as soon as conditions get right again—temperature and humidity and, strangely, the nearness of a host plant— some magic signal is transmitted through the egg-case covering, and the eggs hatch. Nobody knows just what this signal is, but it is selective enough to tell the unhatched eggs that among all the hundreds of thousands of plants on this planet, the one that is *right here* is the right one. Speculation is that each plant root produces its own unique chemical, and this not only triggers the nematode's hatching mechanism, but provides a "chemical road" up which the newly born arachnids travel. The trouble with this theory is that nobody can figure out what good it does the plant. Why would it have ever evolved such a self-destructive characteristic?

Biologists divide nematodes into four groups, depending on what they eat: bacterial feeders, soil-alga feeders, plant-juice feeders, and general predatory feeders—those that live on a variety of living things, like protozoa, fungi, spores, other nematodes.

The plant-juice feeders are the ones that have received the most attention. Naturally. Someone figured that they damage about a half-billion dollars' worth of crops in the U.S. every year. That's two dollars and fifty cents for every person in the country.

One of the commonest nematodes around is the root-knot variety. It attacks roots by injecting them with a solution that causes them to form knots up to a half inch across. While the nematode's eggs are first developing in the female's body, she *feeds* on the knot. Later she lays her eggs—perhaps a thousand of them—inside the knot. It becomes a combination living incubator and food source.

When scientists first turned their lenses onto nematodes they doubted that the innocuous little worms—so soft and tender and harmless looking—could do much real damage. But then they discovered the creature's secret: a built-in toolkit that combines a drill, a hypodermic needle, and a force pump. When the nematode comes across a plump, nutritious root hair, it sticks out a hollow organ from its mouth and bores into the plant. Then, using powerful muscles, it expands an interior bulb which sucks the juices from the root. Finally the muscles squeeze the bulb, forcing the food down into the intestines. The root, meanwhile, slowly shrinks and shrivels like an emptying tube of toothpaste until it is only a shell.

Nematodes have rough lives, though. A variation in soil temperature of only a few degrees will kill some of them. A slight drop in humidity finishes others. An almost unmeasurable change in soil chemistry can wipe out a whole species in an area, making room for a kind that prefers that new condition. Most of all, nematodes need water. Enough moisture must be in an area to coat the soil particles.

Nematodes have all kinds of enemies, some of them pretty strange. But none is weirder than a certain kind of fungus that acts more like an animal than a plant. When nematodes are in the vicinity, this fungus (*Arthrobotrys*) forms itself into a series of loops or rings, something like a mashed ball of chicken wire. The threads are only 1/200 millimeter in diameter, but are as strong as steel.

The unwary nematode comes wriggling along, sticks his head into one of the loops, then suddenly finds himself lassoed. The fungus abruptly expands the loop like an inflating inner tube. The center hole narrows so tightly it strangles the lassoed creature.

Another type of fungus produces loops covered with a sticky substance. As a nematode touches it, he sticks, lashes about, and touches other loops, sticking like a fly to flypaper. The unfortunate animal struggles, then soon is exhausted, then dead.

To feed on the carcass, the fungus sends out a probe, punctures the body, then inserts a sort of drinking straw into the wound. The straw grows, divides, and expands like thread-roots, eventually to fill the entire body as the food substance is digested and sucked back into the fungus. The nematode is eaten inside out. When nothing is left but a hollow shell, the fungus absorbs and digests its own thread-feeders.

A few questions scientists can't quite answer: How can the fungus rings expand rapidly enough to entrap the wiry nematode? How does the fungus kill it? With a chemical injection? And how does the fungus know when nematodes are around? When none are, no rings are formed, and this fungus acts and looks like the ordinary kind.

The nematode-lassoing fungus is only one of the thousands of kinds found in the soil, and the group as a whole performs an extremely important function. Fungi are the principal agents in converting plant matter to soil. Bacteria do the same thing, of course, but fungi tackle material even bacteria won't touch.

Some of the components of wood, for example, are too much for bacteria to handle. But fungi start to work on a downed tree almost immediately, breaking up the wood into smaller pieces, helping the process of decay, adding to the constant turmoil that goes on underground, around the rock.

Fungi do the original cracking so that other things—from bacteria to earthworms—can continue the job. If vegetable matter—leaves, twigs, dead trees—were not broken down, soon the forest would smother in its own remains. It would die from the gradually diminishing nutriments of the soil.

In a pine forest, for example, tons of needles rain down on the floor over the years. The needles are tough. Almost nothing can digest them. Except fungi. They attack newly-fallen needles with gusto, softening them so that animals like the young needle mites can move in to make the needles their home. They continue the cycle of breakdown and the forest is constantly reborn.

Fungi ordinarily are classified as plants—though biologists claim some are animals, or at least something in between. They're usually called plants because of their method of reproduction and general makeup. Except for the fact that they're not green, in most cases they *look* like plants. They never look like animals, though they sometimes act like them.

The big problem in their classification (in addition to the unsettling fact that some of them move about) is that they don't use food in the same way as an ordinary plant. Familiar green plants process by *photosynthesis.* They absorb water and minerals from the earth and carbon dioxide from the air, and with the help of chlorophyll—the substance that makes green plants green—convert the food into the growth material carbohydrate.

Fungi have no chlorophyll (that's why they're not green), and so can't make their own carbohydrate. They get *their* growth food from either living or dead plants or animals. If from living things, they're called parasites—those ledged-shaped fungi you see growing on trees, for instance. If they get their food from dead plants or animals, they're called *saprophytes*—mushrooms, for example. Most are saprophytes.

Fungi in the soil live on such food material as dead roots, moldering insects, live mites, nematodes, and waste matter from such other animals as earthworms.

A year ago last fall I placed a flat rock, about the size of a dishpan, on some newly fallen leaves in the damp woods by my home. By early the next spring a mat of white *mycelium,* the part of a fungus that gathers nutriments, had netted the leaves together with a latticework of white threads. The leaf mass smelled like a damp basement.

By the end of last summer the rotting leaves had begun to resemble the soil beneath the rock. By the end of *this* summer, I was barely able to see the leaves' outlines. Most of the matter had been converted from carbon to carbon dioxide. The rest largely had settled down into the soil.

In the moist, dark conditions under the rock on the hill, a similar fungus grows. This is feeding on the root of a tree that blew down winter before last. The mass of tangle-haired mycelium is made of strings of tiny, elongated cells. Each is microscopic, but when strung together into miles and miles of branched and forked latticework, they look like netting of the finest spider web. They are thriving in the moist rottenness of the old root, removing the starch, sugar, and other foods from the cells.

The fungus net probably started from a minute speck in the soil. It detected potential nourishment, settled on the root surface, then sent out branches which split into reaching fingers. The fingers pushed on, splitting off into more pathways. An advancing branch adds a new finger about every thirty minutes—which in turn branches again a half hour later. Each branch grows at the rate of about a quarter inch a day.

After a time this first species of fungus found chemical conditions changed, so it died off. Shortly later it was replaced by other rot-enhancing fungi that today continue the work. These, too, will be replaced by other species, and later, still others.

The ground under the rock is full of other kinds of fungi. Some specialize in devouring and converting dead insects to earth. Others capture mites in sticky nets and eat them alive. And strangest of all, some kinds of fungi move about like science fiction monsters. These are the mysterious and fascinating slime molds.

Are slime molds plants or animals? You find something that slowly shuffles about like an amoeba, and naturally you classify it as an animal—which is just what a good number of *zoologists* do. But when, next day, your animal has changed into what appears to be tiny mushrooms, you change your mind. You call it a plant—which is what most *botanists* do. Then, being a moderating sort, you reclassify the living bit of matter. You say it is neither. And that's what *mycologists,* those expert in the field of fungi, do.

In the animal stage, the jellylike stage, slime mold is a glint of wet, a glimmer of moist, a touch of shine. It's a blob of white jellyfish undulating along at the breakneck speed of a sick snail. During this part of its life it hides in dark, moist recesses. It's under forest-floor leaves, beneath the rotting bark of fallen logs, and under the rock.

Tip the rock over, look at the undersurface, and if you do find some naked slime mold you won't be terribly impressed. It may be a dot of jelly, or it may be a fan-shaped mass an inch across, but it's not something you want to pick up and cuddle.

In this stage, the *plasmodium*—the name the slime stage is given—crawls about gulping its food whole. Dinner consists in surrounding and absorbing bacteria and yeasts, along with spores and bits of vegetable matter. Almost anything lying in its path.

This glob of pure protoplasm has no cell walls, but dozens of nuclei. Like an enormous amoeba, it squeezes itself into one shape, then the substance flows over itself, doubles about its center, and advances by holding onto earth particles, now with its nose, now with its tail.

One night something signals the smear of goo that time is ripe for reproduction. Maybe food is running low, or the earth beneath the rock is drying, or the temperature is changing. At any rate, the blob feels threatened. It abandons the comfort and security of the cryptosphere and oozes out into the open.

And then, with daylight, comes one of the most remarkable transformations in all of nature. The blob of jelly somehow turns itself into a patch of bizarre flowers—fluffy things on skinny stems wafting in the microwind, or squatty puffballs, or elliptical disks fluttering on slender stalks, or purple, red, and yellow cups, or miniature multi-hued toadstools. Depending on the species—there are at least five hundred of them—and enlarged a thousand times, the patch would make the most spectacular garden on earth.

If, a day after the garden appears, you rub a few of the flowers between your fingers, you'll find a powdery smear of purplish or yellowish dust. This contains the spores, the equivalent of seeds. A breath of wind will carry the spores for miles (some have been found as high as thirty-five thousand feet) to alight and start again the life cycle.

These spores are tough. Some have been germinated after fifty-four years of dry storage, starting to grow within two days of being placed between moist toweling. The spores were typical, and when one "hatched," out swam a farfetched, pear-shaped "swarm cell" equipped with a pair of hairs called *flagella*. These began whipping about like disjointed oars, propelling the naked cell through the miniscule lake formed by moisture between the toweling fibers.

Soon the wandering cell happened to bump against another. Where they touched, the cell walls broke, and they fused into a single, twice-as-large unit. Then the lashing flagella disappeared, and soon the double-size cell began to creep along. It had become a pint-size plasmodium.

As it moved it met other wandering cells. It ate them. And it grew bigger and bigger. Occasionally it met other plasmodia. It merged with these, and it grew still bigger.

If it were in the forest, all this time it would be crawling away from the light, looking for a warm, moist, comfortable place to rest while it gathered energy. It would ooze downward into the soil, splitting into tiny streams of goo to go around sand particles, uniting again and separating again. And all the time it would be gobbling tiny bits of living matter.

Finally, it would get a mysterious call to reproduce—and it would work itself upward again to the space under the bark of a fallen tree, beneath rotting leaves, or under a rock. Which is where we'd find it in the first place.

3. Weather

The climate under the rock is mild, comfortably cool, and moist. In the sheltered world beneath the slab on the New York slope, the temperature and humidity and light vary hardly at all when compared with the rest of the world.

For the delicate organisms of the cryptosphere, the under-rock weather usually is ideal. Occasionally tragedy strikes, but most of the time, as one old naturalist put it, the life is placid and calm—changeless to the point of monotony.

He was wrong. Though the *weather* under a rock is relatively tranquil, life there is in a constant social revolution. Nature is performing her master balancing act between animals and their environment—but one side always seems to outweigh the other.

Under good conditions a certain plant or animal multiplies; but that very act removes those good conditions. Example: A dead mole lies rotting. This is great for fungi (and other organisms) who attack it and flourish wildly. But soon the mole is gone, converted by the fungi into

The climate under the rock remains constant. From left: pill bugs, earthworm, slug, snail.

25

more fungi. Because of lack of food, then, the fungi begin to die. Even as they do, however, fungus-eating bacteria attack them hungrily—and when the fungi are gone, the bacteria, too, die. Then protozoa move in to gobble up the dead bacteria. And so it goes.

The delicate, constantly shifting balance in the world beneath the rock is breathtakingly complex. Tiny elements in the food chain—who are in turn predators and prey— strive for dominance. But no one form of life stays atop for long.

Nevertheless, the rock protects the animals against most abrupt changes, buffers them against the outside world, regulates and moderates the under-rock weather. Just how much it does so I found out a few weeks ago when I decided to see exactly how protective against temperature extremes the hillside rock is. I carefully dug a trench in the soil beneath it and in the opening placed a maximum-minimum thermometer—the kind that tells how hot and cold the air has been since the last time it was set.

I gently replaced the rock, trying not to leave any spaces between the crypt and the outside air. Finally I placed another maximum-minimum thermometer atop the rock.

During the next forty-eight hours the temperature on the rock's surface varied between 58° and 116° F. But under the rock the extremes were only 66° and 94°—and if the rock were thicker, the sheltering effect would have been even greater.

That was in midsummer, in July. Will the same modifying effect be seen during the winter? Probably. But I don't know. Maybe I'll run the experiment next January.

The shielding and cooling effect of the rock is more important than it seems. Unlike larger animals, the creatures of the cryptosphere worry about *too much* heat rather than too little. Birds and mammals usually have a body temperature higher than the air. They are constantly losing heat, even though such insulation as hair and feathers and body fat are designed to keep the heat in.

Crypto-creatures, however, have the situation reversed. They must keep heat out. If they don't, and if the under-rock world gets too hot, their body fluids begin to evaporate; the liquids expand, put pressure on their *exoskeleton*, the tough, protective body covering, burst their blood vessels, and more or less boil out of their skins. They die. So they often live under a shelter rock.

Another source of potential trouble is the heat produced by the organisms themselves. This is the internal energy that comes from activity. The faster one of these tiny animals can rid himself of body heat, the longer he can keep going. One biologist proved this by prodding large spiders until they dropped from exhaustion. He carefully noted the times. Then he did the same thing with smaller spiders. Invariably, he found, the small ones kept going longer. The reason, he determined, is that the smaller animals have a greater ratio of surface to body volume, so they can cool more quickly and keep cool longer.

The rock protects the organisms not only from the sun's heat, but from light. For most plants, light is essential. But it isn't to animals—not even man. In the unprotected outside world, many of the crypto-creatures would last only until an alert bird or toad or lizard spotted them. Under the rock they're safe.

Even more of a danger than predators, however, is the specter of *desiccation,* of drying out. All animals must fight desiccation, but to the creatures under the rock, this is a constant danger. The protective shield of the over-laying slab holds in the dampness—and this is one of the biggest reasons the inhabitants live there.

Sometimes the cover isn't enough. So some of the cryptozoa have evolved elaborate water-saving systems of their own.

Take the pill bug, for instance—a prime example of a water conservationist. The pill bug—also called sowbug or woodlouse—is a 3/8-inch, fourteen-legged creature that looks like a tiny armadillo. You find him any place that's damp and dark, from the Arctic Circle to the Equator—under old boards, beneath cardboard boxes stored in basements, inside rotten logs, under the rock. He's called a pill bug because when you pick him up he'll do one of three things: try to run like mad, faint, or pull in his antennae and legs and roll up in an armor-plated ball, like a pill. (Another story is that old-timers used to pop rolled-up pill bugs into their mouths, living pills for supposed medicinal effects—but somehow I doubt it.)

Another pill bug defense is a row of glands running along each side of his body. When a predator chomps down on him, the glands discharge—and judging from the reaction of the enemy, the fluid tastes awful.

The pill bug himself is supposed to be a vegetarian. But he prefers decaying material, which means that it is heavily coated with bacteria, protozoa, and probably nematodes. And even, sad to say, an occasional baby pill bug. He doesn't notice.

A pill bug is a *crustacean*, one of the few that can live on land. (Other crustaceans include lobsters, crabs, barnacles, and crayfish.) Somehow, hundreds of millions of years ago, he crawled out of the sea. He managed to hang on, but unfortunately, nature hadn't equipped him very well to keep moist. In the first place, tiny things the size of pill bugs lose water quickly—just as they lose heat—because their surface area is large in relation to their volume. Most insects guard against this excessive loss, however, with a waxy body coating that holds the liquids in. Not the pill bug. When he sweats, the water's gone.

Another thing: Pill bugs still have gills—or at least a modified form of them. Gills are terribly inefficient in air, and as a result, pill bugs lose a lot of water simply from breathing.

So how do they survive? By a very curious behavior pattern. When pill bugs find moisture, they automatically tend to slow down, shun light, and walk in circles—or at least to make a lot more turns than normal. Therefore, biologists have found, when humidity is high, the tiny creatures tend to congregate in slowly revolving clumps. This keeps them more or less in moist areas. When the area begins to dry out, though—and even under-rock spots may—the animals become more spirited and move in ever widening circles. Further, the light-avoiding mechanism is shorted out. They don't care if it *is* light; they're interested in trying to find another moist area.

When they do stumble upon one, their light-avoidance switch flips into action again, they get relatively sluggish, and then begin to move in circles again. Until the next dry spell.

For the pill bug and others faced with the constantly pending disaster of drying out, the cryptosphere is about the best place to be. No direct sun penetrates; any moisture present tends to stay there; and no wind dries out moist skins.

Incidentally, if you can't seem to find any pill bugs under the rocks in your area (unlikely), try this: Hollow out a potato and place it beneath a bush, hollow side down. Cover it with leaves to keep the sun from baking it. Or you might try putting one in a damp basement. Two days later you should have some pill bugs living there, for if there's one thing a pill bug loves it's a rotting potato.

One animal even more vulnerable than the pill bug to sunlight and drying is the garden slug. It has learned to hide under a rock or other protection during daylight hours, then to emerge only after sunset to forage for greenery. In the morning, all that's left is a long, winding, glistening trail across dew-moist sidewalks—and a ravaged vegetable garden.

Look for slugs on quiet, warm, moist nights and you'll see multitudes. But check on dry, windy nights, and you'll probably find that they've stayed at home under the rock.

Anatomically, slugs are almost identical with snails (altogether there are some twenty thousand species of these *gastropods*), except that a slug has no external shell. Some kinds of slugs, however, have tiny plates embedded along their backs.

Traveling over his own carpet of mucus, a typical snail or slug finds his way by his two pairs of tentacles, one above the other. The lower two are well-developed organs of touch—like long, flexible fingers with sensitive ends. They help him avoid falling over small obstacles in his path. Good thing, too, because his eyes are looking elsewhere. His tiny eyeballs are on the tips of the upper two tentacles, which are retractile; they can be inverted back into his body when touched, like a submarine periscope or a glove when a finger is withdrawn. He can stretch them out to nearly an inch to see over larger obstacles. Doesn't really matter, though. His eyesight is terrible.

So he relies on his sense of smell, which is pretty good—

sharp enough to lead him unerringly to succulent greens, which he attacks with more than twenty-five thousand microscopic but amazingly effective teeth.

Here are some other things you probably don't know about snails and slugs:

Kansas slugs (*Limax flavus*) may grow to six inches or more.

The majority of snail shells twist to the right (even below the Equator). Why—nobody knows. You can tell which way the twist goes by holding a snail with the shell's pointed end (the apex of the cone) up, and the aperture (the opening out of which the snail's head/foot protrudes) toward you. If the aperture is on your right, the twist is said to be right handed. It looks that way to the snail, too.

Some snails live in the desert. In dry weather they burrow beneath a protective rock and lie there, dormant, sometimes for years, beneath a thick curtain of hardened mucilage, the *epigram*. (This hibernationlike state is called *estivation*.) Then it rains. Suddenly they're alive again. They eat, mate, and two weeks later lay a few dozen eggs (snails are *hermaphrodites;* each possesses both male and female sex organs)—and then, if it's dry again, go back to sleep.

Most snails probably live about ten years, but nobody is certain. One San Francisco woman kept pet snails in her terrarium for four years.

A Massachusetts Institute of Technology professor rigged a harness for snails and found they exert $.40 \times 10^{-6}$ horsepower pulling force. Said in another way: Hook 25 million snails together and they could haul a one-horse shay.

In some scientific circles, arguments rage about how fast snails and slugs can travel. The Royal Ontario Museum of

Zoology puts the speed at 6-1/2 inches a minute—or a mile a week. Scientists at the University of Maryland, however, clocked an "average" snail on a treadmill at only 23 inches an hour. That's only a mile in more than four months. Without sleep.

The great naturalist Charles Darwin once reported a remarkable pair of hungry snails he watched for two days. One snail was "strong," he said, the other, "feeble." The stronger one set out alone, eventually coming upon a good food source in a nearby garden. He returned, claimed Darwin, the next day, presumably bid the other to come along, and the two of them slid off together to the greener pastures.

But enough of snails.

Because snails and other animals of the cryptosphere (and everyone else, for that matter) trace their ancestors back to the sea, the perennial problem facing them is desiccation. But *too much* water can mean trouble, too. Occasionally a flash flood of rainwater, in fact, changes the whole texture of the world under the rock.

A cloudburst swamps the crypt and—panic! Water traps a beetle in a cup of earth and he drowns. Ants wash afloat, then scurry down into the dry reaches of their catacombs. A slug surfaces, trying to keep just above water level. An earthworm wriggles from his burrow—and is plucked away by an earlybird. A corpulent toad, however, sheltering himself from the hot sun of ten minutes ago, now flattens himself in the subterranean puddle, contented as a sow.

The water seeps into the earth beneath the rock, and within a few minutes a cataclysmic change begins to occur. The rain fills the pores between the soil granules, cutting off oxygen from the surface. *Aerobic,* or oxygen-loving bacteria, die, or at least become inactive. In their place *anaerobic* bacteria—those to which oxygen is a poison—move in. (Those are the bacteria responsible for the rotten swamp smell you find when you stir up mud along a lake shore.) The abundant water washes down organic matter, and the bacteria flourish.

Then come the protozoa in swarming hordes to feed on the dying aerobic bacteria. They swim through the newly-created waterways, eating the bacteria and multiplying, eating and multiplying until the game gets scarce. As the rain stops, the earth begins to dry again. Then the protozoa form protective cysts and go back to sleep until next time.

Air, meanwhile, begins to seep down again as the water evaporates or sinks lower. Here and there a lonely aerobic bacterium desperately gulps some oxygen, feeds on a smidge of plant matter, and begins to multiply. The oxygen-hating bacteria begin to die. Soon the mammoths of the cryptosphere—the beetles and the worms and all the others—settle down again to normal living. The flood crisis has passed.

4. Earthworms

If, when you tip up a rock, you see a quantity of earthworms hiding there, you know a number of things. You know the earth is not very acid, for earthworms can't stand sour soil. You know that the ground is honeycombed with worm burrows; when it rains, they act as tiny aqueducts, lessening erosion and allowing water to reach plant roots, and when it doesn't rain, they act as air ducts, letting rich oxygen seep deep into the soil. You know also that plants have an easier time sinking their roots where they have worm passages to follow. And you know that the earth is fairly good there (or else the worms wouldn't be around), and that it is getting richer all the time.

A worm enriches the soil in three ways. First, he hauls leaves and other vegetable matter down below the surface to use as food, where much of it decays. At night, out of sight of birds and the drying rays of the sun, a worm may hang onto his burrow with his rear, bristlelike feet and work around in a circle, like a calf tethered to a post. When he comes to a leaf, he yanks it down into his passage, there to munch at his daytime leisure.

The second way a worm enriches the soil is by his death.

His decaying body adds nutriments to the earth.

The third way—by far the most important—is through his *castings*, little piles of digested soil. According to the United States Department of the Interior, the castings of common earthworms contain an average of five times more nitrogen, seven times more phosphate, and eleven times more potash than the surrounding earth.

A worm divides his burrowing time between shoving himself through the soil like a mole and by eating his way through. When he pushes, he does so by wriggling his pointed snout between the soil particles, then expanding his head, shoving the grains apart. He can stretch like a rubber band, too, because his body is made of one or two hundred semihard rings or segments joined together with softer, stretchable material. He pushes with his feet, four pairs per body segment. And he's strong—stronger for his size, as one researcher puts it, "than any creature which walks, swims, or flies." He also holds the title of World's Largest Invertebrate.

The pushy traveling technique works fine in large-crumb, loose soil, but not so well in compacted earth. In the latter case, a worm finds it easier simply to eat his way.

In essence, a worm is just one long digestive tract. He has no jaw or teeth, but more or less sucks the goodies like a carpet sweeper directly into his muscular throat. Just behind is the *esophagus*. Here the food is given a squirt of liquid from glands lining the esophagus walls. Biologists believe the fluid acts to neutralize acids.

Back a little farther is the leatherlike *gizzard*, which crushes and grinds the food, using sand particles to mash the organic bits until the whole mess is a mushy paste.

What comes out the posterior end, the castings, is a

subtle mixture of nutritive chemicals that makes the very best topsoil. Without earthworms, someone once estimated, nature takes a thousand years to manufacture an inch of topsoil. Worms do it in a decade or less.

One of the first to recognize the worm's worth as a plowman was Cleopatra. Earthworms, she decided, were responsible for the fertility of the Nile Valley, so she ordered them protected and the knowledge guarded as a state secret. A couple of thousand years later came Charles Darwin, who spent years studying the earthworm and his ways. In 1882 he published a book with the uninspiring title *The Formation of Vegetable Mould,* which theorized that if all earthworms disappeared, growing things would decrease almost to the vanishing point—including man.

If earthworms are so good, then, why wouldn't it be wise for a farmer with poor soil to dump thousands of them on his land and let the underground tillers go to work? This was exactly the thinking of a California physiotherapist named Thomas J. Barret when, some years ago, he bought a barren hillside in Los Angeles.

The ground was so poor nothing more than scraggly brush and an occasional cactus would grow. But Dr. Barret transported hundreds of earthworms from nearby fertile valleys and spaded them into the soil with such organic matter as sawdust, manure, garbage, and grass cuttings. And sure enough—soon the hillside scrubland was changed into a miniature Eden, producing flowers and vegetables in superabundance.

Word spread. His story was told in magazines and newspapers and over the air. Other gardeners who tried worms were so impressed they began raising their own and selling the "living fertilizer" to still others. Soon large-scale earthworm farms developed. One Georgia "worm rancher," as he billed himself, was selling something like 35 million worms a year, mainly to farmers.

The worms worked. A gardener would dump a few hundred in his poorly producing plot, and he'd have vegetables galore.

But there was a catch. The following year, or the year after, things would be bad again. What was happening? Any given plot of earth can support only so many worms, and these gardens were already handling all they could. Those worms spaded into the ground that first year simply died, and their bodies gave up valuable nutriments to the plants. But by the next year things were back to normal.

Dr. Barret, on his California hillside, did something largely ignored by the new earthworm enthusiasts; he spaded in organic matter with the worms. So by the time the natural fertilizer had rotted, the soil had been restructured to such a high quality Barret would have been able to grow prizewinning crops anyway. The worms simply changed his production from good to superb.

Further, the worms most people bought through the mail turned out to be fast-breeding "manure" worms (*Eisenia foetida*) raised for fishing—and not terribly good at underground tilling.

Of the Earth's more than two thousand kinds of earthworms, less than a hundred live in the United States. Dr. Gordon E. Gates, earthworm expert and former chairman of the biology department of Colby College, Waterville, Maine, speculates that the cause was the Ice Age. All worms in the northern part of the country were killed off when glaciers swept down from the north, he believes.

Virtually all earthworms you might find under northern rocks, says Dr. Gates, are descendants of those brought over from Europe in the earth surrounding the roots of plants.

Of the worms that never made it over here, some are pretty spectacular. One native of Africa climbs trees. Another, a denizen of the South Seas, becomes furious when picked up, turning himself on like a celebrating fireboat. He squeezes himself and squirts juice from some two dozen portholes in his body, dousing anyone within a yard. Oddest of all are the giant earthworms of the Bass Valley of South Victoria, Australia. These things grow to be eleven feet long and thick as a bratwurst.

Here's how you capture one, according to a native earthworm hunter: Sneak up on him after dusk while he's feeding. Grab him by the head and quickly tie a knot in his body so he can't haul himself back down his burrow. Don't pull, or he'll come apart; let him tire himself trying to slide back down. Then gently ease the monster out inch by inch as he relaxes his grip.

Worms found under most U.S. rocks are usually the common American earthworm *Lumbricus terrestris*, which rarely stretch to more than a foot. Most species reach only half that. What U.S. worms lack in length, however, they make up for in quantity: Earthworms under an ordinary farm pasture may weigh twice as much as the cattle grazing above. Darwin calculated that an acre may contain fifty thousand earthworms. His estimate was way low. Some counts since have placed the ordinary population in the neighborhood of a million or so, and in one spot in New Zealand, transported European earthworms flourished so well that one soil-research station recorded a density of 4.3 million worms per acre in pastures.

The individual earthworm whiles away his time eating, mating, and escaping from danger. Though he has no eyes, his skin is so sensitive to light that the first glimmer of dawn sends him slipping downward—long before harsh sunrays begin to dry him. He has no ears, but his sense of touch is so fine that the sound of a shrew's footsteps dispatches him into his burrow. If a mole snips off his tail—as much as 4/5 of him, in fact—he'll regenerate a new one. Decapitate him, though, and he may or may not be able to grow a new head. If too many segments are lost—say, more than a dozen—he may be able to grow only a new tail where his head should be. Trouble.

When a heavy rain comes, the worm panics. He doesn't really mind the water, but he does need oxygen, and rain may cut off the supply. If the ground is soft enough, he rushes downward in a mad dash to find air. If he finds the ground too hard, he has no choice but to turn around and squirm upward, up, up to the atmosphere, whether or not the ground is covered with water. One old naturalist reported that on a late fall day he once found a clutch of earthworms atop a compacted layer of snow about eight inches thick. He couldn't understand at first, because a worm's sensitive skin requires warmth. But then he realized that the ground temperature was above freezing, and melting snow was cutting off the worms' oxygen. They had crawled up through the snow to breathe.

Actually, desiccation is a problem more common than drowning. And that's why worms are so often found under rocks. Moisture condenses on a rock's underside and forms the community wetpatch. A cross section of the land around a rock would look something like a road map of a desert city: All roads lead to it.

Incidentally, nobody knows for sure how long worms

ordinarily live. One biologist speculates that three or four years is probably the natural life span, but that the length might be doubled in captivity. This is a good area for easy, long-term research.

When days shorten toward winter, earthworms migrate —straight down. Zoologist Walter J. Harman, when he was at Louisiana State University, once opined that "ten feet is generally cited as the depth to which they will penetrate. But I suspect that the labor of digging them at greater depths lessens the search."

At any rate, in the fall a worm burrows down to somewhere below the frost line. And there he mingles with dozens of his cohorts in a slimy, slippery ball, the better to save his skin moisture through the long winter. When spring brings the thaw, disintegrating the ball of worms, each animal hungrily squirms off for a postwinter meal and a little sex.

Worms are hermaphroditic, which makes things in that area easier all around. They don't breed all by themselves, however. They cross-fertilize, and produce two broods—certainly a system more efficient than most. The couple snuggles up, toes to nose, and each grabs hold with his/her bristlelike feet and copulates. Sometimes all night.

Earlier, in anticipation of the mating, a plasticlike girdle, a *clitellum,* had formed around the body of each about a quarter back from the head. (Maybe three-quarters of the mature worms you find have clitella.) Now the girdle hardens, and gradually slides forward along the body, picking up in it the eggs of one parent, the sperm of the other, and a little nutritive material, like the white of an egg. Finally the case slips off, the ends snap together, and it becomes a greenish, rice grain-size protector for the half dozen or so young growing inside.

One end of the case hardens, but the other stays semi-soft—so the young can get out when they're ready. The babies usually develop for about a month, but may stay in the case over winter, and have been kept viable in the laboratory for two years without any apparent damage.

A baby worm—white when he first emerges—eats like a maniac and grows astonishingly fast. Under good conditions he'll be big enough to mate in three or four months. When once he matures he'll produce a clitellum every week or so in the warm months. And all the time he's acting, as Aristotle said, as "the intestines of the earth."

"It may be doubted whether there are many other animals," wrote Darwin, "which have played so important a part in the history of the world as have these creatures." They're literally digesting the earth—silently, secretly serving all nature.

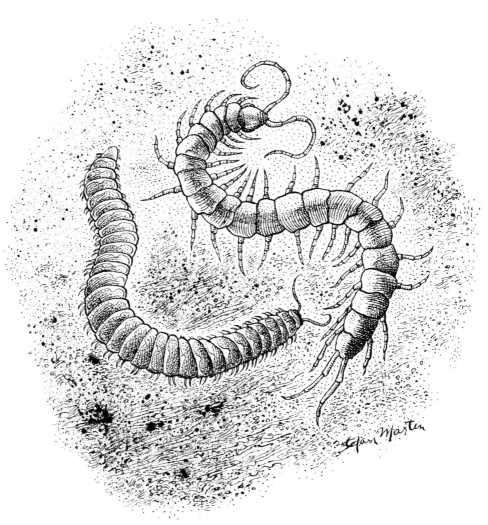

5. The 'Pedes

Ever since I was a kid centipedes have frightened me. Pick one up? Never. Because they sting.

Or do they? Frankly, a couple of months ago I didn't know. Even after consulting authorities. The worst you could expect from a bite, according to one noted biologist, is a sting hardly more painful than from a mosquito, or at most, a spider. Another authority, however—an equally expert expert—cited instances of horrendous pain and paralysis. And E. Laurence Palmer, in his famous (and excellent) *Fieldbook of Natural History,* says centipede poison "will kill many small animals, but isn't dangerously harmful to man, though it may be painful." Then he adds, not very reassuringly, "Treat by bathing in ammonia solution and retarding blood flow."

I never actually knew anyone suffering from an American centipede bite. Certainly *I* hadn't been bitten. Only one way to find out, I figured. Get bit.

I lifted up the hillside rock, spotted an inch-long centipede scurrying off, clumped a small goldfish net over him, and transferred him to a tiny pill bottle. My plan was to induce him to bite me. Original research.

But first I stretched flat on my back in full sunlight, and with a magnifying lens held to my eye, examined my captive through the side of the bottle. His legs moved in waves, like cilia, like fields of wheat in the wind. The sun lit up his body like a piece of neon amber—and enlarged, he looked like a toy. I half expected to see the outline of gears and motors through his plastic body segments.

He stopped running long enough for me to get a good look at his twenty legs, each pair attached to a segment. They were oddly jointed and pointly, like telescoping tripod legs. Actually, there *should* have been twenty, but two had been lost in the net. Centipedes, I found, are delicate.

Two translucent, golden antennae, half as long as the centipede's body and seemingly made of strings of beads, jutted from his head, and as I looked he bent each in turn and drew it through his gash of a mouth, wiping it clean.

That mouth was appalling: ghastly in close-up. Crossed just in front, like a weird moustache, were two tiny, tusk-like claws. Through these, I knew, flowed the poison. *Those* would bite into me?

Ten seconds later they did. And I was almost disappointed. The sting, if you could call it that, was simply a sharp tick, the equivalent of a squeeze between the fingernails. It didn't even break the skin. Relief.

Later I ran across an apparently authentic case of a centipede of a different species having bitten a seven-year-old Philippine girl on the head. She died twenty-nine hours later. But the one that bit me proved only that he could.

Millipedes, on the other hand, are missing those fangs. Rather than attack, a millipede curls himself into a tightly wound spiral if picked up, hoping whatever is bothering him will go away—a characteristic shared with armadillos, pill bugs, and some human beings.

Both millipedes and centipedes have another peculiar trait shared by other crypto-creatures: a *tropism,* or involuntary movement, known as *thigmotaxis.* This is a desire to have solid, physical contact on as many sides as possible when in danger. A beetle feels this need when he scurries under bark, a mouse feels it when he wedges himself beneath a rock, and even a possum feels it when, pursued, he scrunches down in thick grass, hiding. They all are reassured by the tactile closeness of cover.

Sometimes, however, millipedes just don't care. Dr. J. L. Cloudsley-Thompson, an English zoology lecturer at King's College in London, tells of cases of mass migration of the creatures out in the open sunlight. He says they have stopped railway trains. So many of them were squashed on the tracks the locomotive couldn't get traction, and sand finally had to be strewn on the rails before the driving wheels could grip. On other occasions, he reports, "cattle have refused to graze on invaded pastures, wells have been filled with drowned corpses and workmen cultivating the fields have become nauseated and dizzy from the odor of millipedes crushed by their hoes."

Millipedes and centipedes belong to the class Myriopoda, which means ten thousand feet in Greek—a classic Aegean exaggeration. They belong to separate orders (centipedes are Chilopoda, millipedes, Diplopoda), and differ in a number of ways:

Most centipedes are flat; most millipedes, cylindrical or tubular.

Centipedes have long legs, millipedes, usually short. So a centipede moves fast—swift as a cockroach; a millipede, slow—slow as a trotting ladybug.

All fifteen hundred species of centipede (two hundred of them in the U.S.) have a single pair of legs on each body segment. Millipedes have two on each.

When either animal walks across the ground he constantly taps the surface in front of him with his antennae to test it; tiny sensory hairs and chemoreceptors on the tips tell him about such things as hardness, moisture, texture, and acidity.

Some centipedes (which means hundred-legged) have more than two hundred pairs of legs, while others stumble about on only a dozen or so. Though millipede means "thousand-legged," they never do quite make it. Prize for the maximum number so far found goes to a twenty-three-inch Tobago millipede (*Siphonophora millepeda*) found by diplopodologist H. F. Loomis of Miami, Florida, in 1932. Loomis counted 740 legs (give or take a dozen) sticking out from 192 segments. A close runner-up is a fourteen-inch California monster called *Illacme plenipes,* which trots along on 732 legs.

Another point of difference between the 'pedes is food. Mild-mannered millipedes are vegetarians. Their favorite: tree leaves being attacked by fungi. Since millipedes apparently lack enzymes necessary to break down cellulose, most of their sustenance must come from cellulose-lacking fungi, or partially broken-down leaves. Because of this fondness for vegetable matter, millipedes perform a great service on the forest floor. They help break down litter and make it more vulnerable to fungal and bacterial action, so its richness can return to the soil. Millipedes are extremely touchy eaters, by the way. They often will refuse to munch on the leaves of anything but one particular subspecies of tree—and sometimes only leaves from certain parts of the tree.

Centipedes, on the other hand, are purely carnivorous, and not picky at all. Their favorite dish seems to be insects and larvae, garnished with earthworms. The common house centipede (*Scutigera forceps*) found in damp basements, lives mainly on such pests as silverfish and cockroaches, so from man's point of view, he's beneficial. One cockroach a week seems to be enough to make an average U.S. centipede happy. One huge individual of *Scolopendromorpha gigas*, a native of Trinidad, was kept in the Insect House of the Zoological Society of London for more than a year. Its meals consisted mainly of "small mice, which it devoured with alacrity," as the report read.

The poison fangs, of course, are used for hunting. A centipede rushes up and pounces on his victim, plunges the set of pincerlike hypodermics into him, then injects the venom, which, if it doesn't kill the prey outright, certainly does make him unhappy.

What makes a *centipede* unhappy are the natives of parts of Polynesia. They roast the local hot-dog-size centipedes over small fires, then with zest devour all but head and rump. Toads eat millipedes. Seventy-seven were found in the stomach of one American toad. And birds—starlings especially—love them. One study revealed that in April, millipedes made up 55 percent of the diet of starlings in a typical locale.

Most female centipedes (all myriopods have separate sexes) simply lay their eggs in damp earth and forget about them. But one straw-colored Mediterranean species (*Scolopendra cingulata*) has a rather remarkable way of protecting her offspring-to-be. First, under a large, flat rock, she digs a depression about the size of a ping pong ball. Then into it she lays some two dozen eggs. Now, very gently, she encircles them with her body, winding herself, legs tucked in, so carefully that no eggs can be seen. She stays wound up like that for nearly a month, until the young are several days old. During this time she hardly moves except occasionally to open her coil and lick the eggs, apparently protecting them from fungus.

Most millipedes also roll up into balls. But they do it to protect *themselves,* not their eggs. Just how good the defense is was determined in 1967 by Dr. Thomas Eisner, Cornell University entomologist. When he tossed large (3/4 inch in diameter), rolled-up African millipedes to various predatory animals—a blue jay, ants, a mouse, a mongoose—in all cases but one the millipedes were safe. The jay pecked at his, but it bounced away unhurt. The mouse tried to bite one, but the shell was too smooth. The ants swarmed all over theirs, trying to bite into it, Eisner reports, "but with the millipede's legs and antennae inaccessibly tucked away, the ants could not secure the necessary hold."

Then Eisner rolled one to the mongoose, a banded variety that, like the millipede, came from Africa. "The predator responded instantly," he wrote, "sniffing it, and rolling it about with the paws." The mongoose tried to bite his prey, but no luck. Then suddenly he dropped the morsel from his jaws and picked it up with both front paws, "The mongoose backed against a rocky ledge in the cage, assumed a partially erect stance, and—with a motion so quick as to be barely perceptible—hurled the millipede backward between its legs, smashing it against the rocks." Then he ate it.

The reason the mongoose so easily cracked the secret of the millipede, Eisner suspects, is that millipedes make up a natural part of the diet of mongooses in their native Africa.

An even more interesting millipede trait—at least of a particular kind (*Apheloria corrugata,* abundant around Ithaca, N.Y.)—was discovered by the same Dr. Eisner in 1963. His curiosity was aroused when he placed one of the creatures near a colony of ants he keeps in his laboratory. The ants rushed upon it, he reported, "biting its legs with their mandibles, and otherwise assailing it from all quarters."

But strangely, the millipede didn't try to run. Instead, he came to an abrupt halt, tucked his head beneath his body, and waited. "Next a dramatic thing happened," wrote Eisner. "The entire ant swarm suddenly dispersed, the individual ants fleeing aimlessly in all directions." When the ants were gone, the millipede ambled off, unconcerned.

Next, Dr. Eisner offered a millipede to a toad—a notorious millipede gourmand. The toad promptly switched out his sticky tongue and flicked the animal into his mouth. But he didn't swallow it. "In what amounted to a most grotesque gesture," Eisner reported, "the toad spit out the millipede, and in obvious discomfort was left 'pawing' his tongue with his front feet."

Clearly, these millipedes were able to produce some chemical that was repulsive to predators. But what?

A glint of answer came when someone on Eisner's staff remembered that years ago naturalists used certain kinds of millipedes in insect "killing jars." You put a few millipedes in a bottle, then toss in insects or other tiny creatures, and soon everybody but the millipedes is dead. Another colleague recalled that natives of central Mexico grind up one species with various plants to make poison for their arrows.

More of the answer was revealed when Eisner noticed

that whenever he annoyed a millipede—roughed him up a bit—then sniffed him, he could detect a faint odor of bitter almonds. Ah ha!

Now he knew what the poisonous substance was. But he had to prove it. If it was what he thought, the millipede must be mixing two chemicals together to evolve the poison. "The obvious thing to do next was to examine the anatomical apparatus responsible," he said. So carefully, under a microscope, he cut into the tiny ducts lining the animal's side—two of them on each body segment. Inside he found two sacs joined by a narrow duct closed by a springlike valve or trapdoor. In each was a different liquid.

"In order to envison how the gland effects its discharge," he later explained, "one need only imagine the simultaneous occurrence of two things: compression of the [innermost] reservoir, and contraction of the muscle that controls the valve. The result is obvious."

When the millipede squeezes himself, he squirts one chemical into another, then both into the air. What comes out into the mouth of a predator is as nearly a universal poison as one can find: cyanide.

One question remains. When the millipede discharges its numerous sacs of poison it is immersed in noxious fumes. How is it that the creature doesn't keel over from its own product? "How does it cope," asks Eisner, "with the cyanide that must inevitably seep into its body through the respiratory system?" So far, nobody knows.

—as it was with the millipedes—so he tried an experiment. He glued a cockroach to a piece of paper, then placed the paper in front of a laboratory ant colony. The ants rushed out and started biting the roach, and "the roach responded instantly by ejecting the spray," Eisner reported. Pow. The ants recoiled and went rushing back to their nest again, with "a series of abnormal seizures, during which leg movement became discoordinated and ineffectual, hampering and sometimes halting locomotion."

The trick doesn't always work, though. Eisner tried the same thing using praying mantises as the predators, and, as he reported, the mantises "seemed to be completely unaffected by the spray, and every roach seized was invariably devoured."

So far as the roach's spreading of disease is concerned, that still is open to question, though there is some indication that roaches harbor salmonella, food-poisoning bacteria. The truth probably is that they rarely carry germs in their systems like mosquitoes and rats do, but because the domestic varieties do tramp through human filth, they track around bacteria responsible for intestinal disorders, and some viruses as well.

However, as one roach defender (there *are* a few) put it: "It is one thing to prove that the roach carries disease organisms—quite another to prove that he actually spreads disease." Admits a United States Government health agent: "We can't pin anything on him."

Actually, the roach himself is a fastidious little animal. In that pill bottle in which I entrapped the two under the rock, the insects spent about half the time trying to escape, the other half cleaning themselves.

People who live with multitudes of roaches, however—

ghetto dwellers, for the most part—have a worry other than disease. They are often troubled with roach allergy. Insects in the walls can cause skin eruptions, symptoms similar to hay fever and asthma. And the insects needn't even be around, researchers have found. Explains Dr. Alfred V. Zamm, Kingston, N.Y., allergist: "You would be amazed at the enormous quantity of American packaged foods that carry bits and pieces of insects, especially roaches. It's probable that no American escapes eating them to some degree. And those sensitive to them are bound to suffer."

Roaches are in the flour because they're in the mills— one of their better homes. Other American varieties (there are fifty-three of them) live everywhere from the desert to above the Arctic Circle, from deep in caves to under woodland rocks. All are members of the huge Blattidae family, part of the Orthoptera order, which includes grasshoppers, crickets, and locusts. Most notorious are the domestic roaches—the huge, mahogany-colored American, found in basements and other damp places; the fleet-footed German Roach or Croton Bug, lover of apartment houses; the inch-long, dark brown, and shiny Oriental; the squat Brown-banded, a tropical roach that somehow favors military installations.

But you rarely find any of these out in the field. Some that you *do* are as tiny as wheat grains; others, as large as a finger, their wings spreading to seven inches or more. All roaches have wings of some sort, but most can't use them very well. When I tossed one of my pets into the air he buzzed to earth like a windup glider, disappearing into the leaves as soon as he touched.

The other one I placed in a petri dish, then studied him with a magnifying glass. He was, I later determined, the Pennsylvania Wood Roach (*Parcoblatta pennsylvanica*), probably our most abundant native species. In appearance he resembled a multitude of others, and in close-up even a roach is stunning. His flattened body (designed for zipping into hairline cracks) glowed golden in the sunlight, and his long, whispy antennae, feathered with downy hair, waved amber. Longer than the roach himself, the feelers act as a nose and probably ears as well, and they help him find his way around the perpetual nighttime of the rock's underside.

His eyes help, too, of course, but only when a little light seeps into the cryptosphere. When it does, they are excellent for detecting movement. And that's another prime reason why the family of roach is so long-lived. He slizzles away before a predator can attack.

Two tiny antennae at the rear of his shell, the *cerci,* also help him flee cockroach eaters. The cerci are covered with hairs which bend in the wind, and they are extraordinarily sensitive to minute vibrations in the air. The message conveys itself directly to his six powerful legs without any time wasted on brainwork.

To find out just how quickly a roach can react, Professor Kenneth Roeder of Tufts University in Medford, Mass., rigged up a device that would direct a stream of air simultaneously at a roach's tail and at a little flag alongside him. He stuck the roach on a tiny treadmill, and attached both the track and the flag to a recording device. Whenever he blew at the roach's rear, the flag would record the moment the air struck it, and the roach would record how much later *he* reacted. The answer: an incredible average of 1/20 of a second.

Ability to escape predators isn't the only reason the roach has been around so long. Another one is that he's exceedingly tough. You can freeze him, step on him, shoot him with enough radiation to kill a herd of bison—and if left alone he'll likely skitter away unscathed. He can survive at least seventy-six days on water alone, three weeks without food *or* water, and he can go nearly a week without even his head. DDT and its early sisters hardly bother the household varieties anymore, and the chemical industry is forced to work overtime producing new biocides, more and more deadly.

Roaches are smart, too. Scientists first realized his IQ back in 1912 when C. H. Turner, one of the top black biologists of the time, taught roaches to run mazes, an intelligence measuring system usually reserved for higher animals.

The maze, in the biology lab of Sumner Teachers College in St. Louis, consisted of a bewildering complex of narrow copper pathways passing over a basin of water. Most of the wound-about paths ended in blind alleys. But one led, in a complicated pattern, to the roach's home—dark, snug, cozy.

Turner found that after only five or six tries at half-hour intervals, most roaches would be running the maze faster and making fewer errors, an astonishing feat for an insect. And at the end of the day the mistakes were reduced virtually to zero. The scientist also made note of—but chose not to comment on—the fact that the males learned faster than the females.

Another factor in the longevity of the cockroach is his sex drive; he'd rather mate than eat. Not so with most other animals. Rats, for instance, want water, food, and sex, in that order. And if they're low on food, they're not much interested in sex. A hungry cockroach, on the other hand, apparently is even *more* interested in sex than a full one.

Incidentally, baby roaches can (but rarely do) come from females that were never fertilized. The young are always females, and the process is *parthenogenesis.*

A typical woodland roach—of whatever parentage—starts life inside an egg (one of perhaps a dozen or two) that is in turn inside a brown or tan sausage-shaped sack, an *ootheca* (pronounced oh'-ah-the'ka). The ootheca usually is carried for a few days or weeks protruding from mama's posterior. Then she sticks it to the underside of a rock, or buries it in the sand, or perhaps sets it in a rotten-spongy portion of a log.

Some time later (from two weeks to a couple of months, depending on the species) the young—tiny, pale, near-wingless nymphs—hatch first from eggs, then from the ootheca. Man enters the world ignorant of virtually everything he needs to know; a cockroach, like other insects, is born with complete knowledge of virtually everything he must do for the rest of his life.

The young roaches grow fat on a variety of foodstuffs —moldering plants, carcasses of other creatures, fungi, nearly anything they can get their mouths around. They molt, grow larger, and at the last molt emerge with fully developed wings. The molting process varies from a couple of months in the field roach to about a year in the wood roach.

When they are old enough to mate—some twenty-four hours after the final molt—the female exudes a powerful perfume proclaiming her readiness, and males come galloping from all over to take her up on the idea. The first one there rubs her antennae with his, then announces his intentions to any other male who happens to have the same idea. He often does this by butting an adversary, but when pressed may resort to snipping off a leg.

Soon the winning male turns his back on the female, and lifts his wings. She climbs atop him and they copulate for anywhere from a couple of minutes to two hours or more. Then, in a week or two, the female gives birth. By the end of her life—from a few months to a couple of years —a typical female roach can be responsible for adding thousands of youngsters to the world.

All these qualities—high birth rate, intelligence, and especially toughness—make the cockroach one of the most durable creatures in the world. And as a 1965 newspaper advertisement placed by the National Committee for a Sane Nuclear Policy pointed out, he may outlive us all. "A nuclear war, if it comes, will not be won by the Americans . . . the Russians . . . the Chinese," stated the ad. "The winner of World War III will be the cockroach."

7. The Under-Rock Community of Crickets, Spiders, Beetles

Carefully lift a rock from the soil, and where stone meets earth you'll find a subterranean road network. The rock on the New York hillside is typical. Earthworms were the prime road builders there—eating paths through the soil where the rock rested on it—and from these main thoroughfares, beetles and bugs and ants and multitudes of other creatures carried out or pushed aside or trampled down the dirt to make tiny lanes. Today, if you look closely, the network of paths resembles a road map.

One creature particularly adept at road building is the cricket.

Where the cockroach is nearly universally detested, the cricket is loved. Not because he's helpful to man (he isn't) or outstandingly beautiful (a cockroach outshines him by far) or even because he has a particularly interesting personality. He's loved because he can chirp. And that chirping represents probably the oldest acoustical

From top center, moving clockwise: daddy-long-legs, wolf spider, click beetle, cricket, Hercules beetle.

communications system still extant, dating back to before the Jurassic Period of dinosaurs, some 200 million years ago.

Just after dusk one sultry July evening I caught a cricket in the midst of his concert. Spotlighted in the beam of my flashlight—red cellophane stretched over the lens—he squatted in a little cave at the edge of the rock, a cricket-size burrow he had dug.

At first the half-hidden animal—a Black or Field Cricket (*Gryllus assimilis*), America's most common—sat silent, cautious because of the noise of my approach. But after five minutes of immobility he shrugged, lifted his wing covers over his back at a 45° angle, slid one over the other, and fluttered them. The underside of each wing cover is equipped with a thick vein with a filelike edge of one hundred or more teeth. On the upperside of each wing cover is a hard scraper. When he rubbed file against scraper (most of the time right over left), the shrill *creeak, creeak, creeak* that came from the wing-membrane sounding board seemed impossibly loud. Under good conditions a cricket's call (one hundred decibels at a few inches) can be heard a mile away.

The insect was a male—only the males sing—and he was telling any female cricket who cared to know, how to find him in the dark.

Any cricket who happened to have heard him did so through its knees or shinbones—because that's where crickets' ears are located. Interestingly, to most insects the world is silent. Some detect echoes and other vibrations by special pressure-sensitive organs. But only locusts, cicadas, most moths, grasshoppers, and crickets hear by means of eardrums—the kind of tympanic membranes human beings have.

For a time, however, some entomologists doubted that crickets were really hearing those calls. In at least one case, in fact, they seemed to be totally deaf. A New Jersey cricket buff, intrigued with the apparent fact that some crickets chirp in unison, began to wonder about the possibilities of leading a fieldful of them in concert with the aid of a mechanical chirper.

So he devised an elaborate electronic noisemaker, adjustable to a wide range of frequencies and rhythms.

It sounded pretty good—virtually indistinguishable from the real thing. At least it did to him. Not, apparently, to crickets. He and a couple of friends set the thing up in a Jersey meadow in which crickets already were chirping, turned it on full blast, and adjusted it through its whole range.

But nobody paid the slightest attention.

It was only long afterward, when he discussed his experience with an English cricket expert, that he learned that the animals aren't really listening to the sounds we human beings hear, but to frequencies high in the ultrasonic ranges. The noise we hear is only incidental to the cricket. The experimenter's equipment had produced sounds that to crickets were meaningless.

Evidence that crickets really do communicate by chirp was later shown by a simple experiment. Researchers put females in one soundproof box, males in another, then connected the two by a high-quality intercom system. When the males chirped, the females crowded around the receiver trying to find them. So that was that.

Most crickets vary their call pulses with the temperature, and some—particularly the snowy tree cricket (a kind that chirps in unison)—do it so constantly you can get a fairly accurate reading by counting the chirps and applying a simple formula. Legend has it the method was worked out in 1897 by a physicist who happened to be spending a short time in the Ft. Madison, Iowa, jail. During the course of endless nights he noted what apparently was a change in cricket chirp rate between cold and hot nights. With the aid of a borrowed thermometer he discovered that if he counted the chirps in fifteen seconds and added 38 his answers were rather close to the temperature in degrees Fahrenheit.

Someone else found that the snowy cricket's *pitch* also raises with the temperature. At 70° F. he chirps in F sharp below middle C. To hit middle C itself, the temperature must reach 86°.

Crickets sing for a variety of reasons, entomologists recently have found, not only romantic ones. They chirp to establish their territory, to proclaim danger, to warn rivals, or simply to hear themselves talk. During these times they use only about half of the teeth on their files.

When they become earnest about mating, however, they start using about 90 percent of their sounding strip, varying the stroke with the degree of passion. As Anna Botsford Comstock put it in her classic 1911 *Handbook of Nature-Study*, "The cricket's note has a wide range of expression. When waiting for his ladylove, he keeps up a constant droning; if he hears his rival, the tone is sharp and defiant; but as the object of his affection approaches, the music changes to a seductive whispering, even having in it an uncertain quiver, as if his feelings were too strong for utterance."

When his intended finally hops up, ready, she lets him know with a loving nudge or two. She has recognized him by his call, distinctive to the species. He stops his song, lifts his wings, and she climbs upon his back. She locates a pair of tiny depressions just in back of his wing joints, two cups filled with a secretion she finds mouth-watering. She munches the substance for a half hour or so, then the two of them settle down to the serious business of mating.

One way to tell the female from the male is in the size of the wing covers. The male's are considerably larger—the better to call with. An easier way, though, is to check for a long, thin, *ovipositor* sticking out from the end of the female's abdomen. The male has none.

Late in the summer or early in the fall the female uses this ovipositor to lay a few hundred eggs—some in bunches, others singly—in crevices in the ground. They hatch either that fall or early next spring, and the tiny crickets emerging are small, wingless, pale imitations of their parents. It will be midsummer before the young males have wings developed highly enough for strumming.

Some kinds never do. The Camel or Cave Cricket (*Ceuthophilus gracilipes*), for instance, not only is missing the necessary wings, but ears as well. But then this common under-rock dweller is more closely related to grasshoppers (family Tettigonidae) than true crickets (family Gryllidae) anyway, and doesn't look much like either one of them. He's somehow deformed, like a cricket that ran into a wall so hard his head was pushed backward, his back painfully humped.

For those who go in for offbeat pets, both the camel variety and the field cricket adapt themselves admirably to life in a terrarium. An Australian import—a fast-breeding, tough individual—is being raised commercially in the South for fishermen. One Memphis dealer claims that at any one time he usually is raising about 15 million crickets in his five huge breeding buildings, feeding them some five tons of chicken mash a day.

On a somewhat smaller scale, a half-dozen crickets in a woodland terrarium made from an old five-gallon aquarium, or even a large jar, will do nicely on melon and other sweet, juicy fruits, sliced potatoes, oatmeal dampened with milk, or bread sprinkled with stale beer. And the pets will fill the home with song.

Spiders have had a bad press. The name itself brings to mind an aggressive insect ready to pounce on and bite anyone who happens to pass. Wrong. Spiders aren't insects, they're rarely aggressive, and anything much larger than themselves terrifies them.

Further, from man's viewpoint, they're good. They kill insects in enormous quantities, and they don't do it by flooding the landscape with deadly chemicals. A spokesman for the National Pest Control Association of Elizabeth, N.J., says probably no other group, including birds, eliminates insects in "such astronomical total tonnage" as spiders. Other experts go so far as to claim that without spiders human life couldn't exist. In a spiderless world insects would multiply so fast the earth would be stripped of plant life. Each year, someone else estimated, spiders consume insects equal in weight to the entire human population of earth.

So let's hear no more antispider talk.

Instead, let me tell you about a battle I saw late this past summer between a spider and one of my personal and perennial enemies, a paper wasp. The spider was an Ariadna (*Ariadna bicolor*), a purplish-brown creature with pale sides, not quite a half inch long. She had built her funnel-shaped web along the side of the rock, attached between it, a dead oak seedling, and a milkweed stem. Her retreat hole—the funnel center—was secluded underneath the side of the rock, in the space between it and the ground.

Not twenty seconds after I first noticed the web, a wasp stumbled over one of the outlying threads, and while he was gathering his aerodynamic balance, blundered full tilt into the main part of the structure. Temporarily he was caught in the web's stickiness.

The network shook, sending the message of capture to its builder. Instantly the Ariadna came bounding out—but stopped short, not quite so sure she was happy with her mammoth captive.

She considered the struggle vibrations for a moment (spiders are so nearsighted they can tell the size of a captive better through their webs than their eyes), decided the animal wasn't too large after all, and pounced.

With three pairs of her legs she grabbed one of her bewildered victim's legs, twisted him over, sank her poison fangs into his side, and whipped a strand of silk around him. Then she zipped back into her lair for a moment of rest. It all happened so fast the wasp hardly had time to think of retaliation. And by the time he did, she was gone, and he was left humped nearly double, stinging the air.

Had the insect been too large, the spider would have cut it from the web, letting it drop to the ground—to guard against the web's being demolished. The wasp also would have been cut out if it tasted bad—as do certain moths, flies, and beetles. Most of *these* insects don't struggle when caught, but instinctively lie still, waiting for the spider to bite. When she does, the taste is so awful she wipes her mouth on a leaf, then gets rid of the offending insect. He

drops to the ground and likely survives. If he had strug-
gled, the spider might have poisoned first and tasted
later.

The act of poisoning—particularly the activation of the
poison glands—is the trigger that sets off a spider's spinning mechanism to produce the swathing, or insect-retain-
ing, band. This particular thread is unique; it is broad and
thick, composed of tough, parallel strands that roll out
from one set of *spinnerets* (web-thread glands), and a
crisscross jumble of sideways fibers from another spinneret set. This reinforced thread is amazingly strong—
considerably stronger in some species than steel, in fact.

The wasp was still thrashing in the Ariadna's web, so
the little spider rushed out again, chomped down on his
abdomen, and whipped another few bands around him.
Then she rushed back to her hole again.

A half minute later, the wasp was continuing to struggle, but not so wildly. The spider again trotted out,
wrapped a few more strands around the larger animal, and
again retreated.

By the time an hour had gone by, the wasp was either
dead or paralyzed, and the spider nonchalantly wandered
over, crunched down with her muscular mouth, and dined,
injecting powerful digestive juices and sucking out the
liquefied insides—"drinking" her dinner, as a spider must.

Over the next three days the wasp shrunk and shrunk
as his liquid interior gradually was pumped dry. Finally,
nothing was left but a shriveled, shrunken sliver of tissue
hardly larger than this dash —.

What *is* this thing called a spider, that looks like an insect but isn't? Like insects and crustaceans, it belongs to
the large phylum Arthropoda, animals with a hard outer

skeleton and jointed legs. More specifically, a spider is an arachnid, as are scorpions, daddy-longlegs, and mites. Spiders (and other arachnids) differ from insects in that the head and thorax are grown together in what is called a *cephalothorax*—which contains not only the brains, but the stomach. And it's to this that all the legs—eight, not six —are attached. Further, arachnids have no antennae.

Unlike insects, which have large compound eyes, most spiders have from one to four pairs of bright, simple eyes on the top of the head. (Some, however—cave dwellers, principally—have none at all.) No spider has wings. While not all can spin webs, all can produce silken strands of one kind or another.

Almost all spiders produce poison to some extent, but except in very rare instances, the venom is virtually harmless to human beings, and usually the fangs are so small and feeble they can't break through human skin anyway.

Spiders have no ears as such, but their legs are extremely sensitive to vibrations—and, some scientists say, to sound. Entomologists at Harvard found that certain spiders are somehow attuned to special notes. When a certain musical tone is sounded, they're so upset they drop to the ground—whether in ecstasy or outrage no one can tell.

On the other hand, a highly poisonous burrow-making Australian spider (*Selenocosmia crassipes*) makes a noise himself. He barks—or at least makes a sound like a bark. He does it by the equivalent of gnashing his teeth—by scraping bristly structures on his jaws against tough pegs on other parts of his mouth. The sound is something like that made by rubbing a comb against a table leg, or by pouring BB's into a heavy plate from four inches. The sound is not a love call; probably no other spider can hear it. Likely it's a defense mechanism, a threat heard only by animals with ears.

A spider's ears—as well as her nose, fingers, eyes to a large extent, home, and highway—is her web, a nonliving extension of herself. The web comes from seven different types of glands (not all present in all spiders) that lead to the open air through the spinnerets, and each gland secretes a different kind of thread. In addition to the tough, multilayered swathing band, spiders may spin firm, strong, main scaffolding strands used to build the web support cables; sticky, elastic threads upon which victims ensnare themselves; fine strings the spider plays out when she drops from one height to another, and up which she can climb to safety; and others used only for such things as egg sacs, lair casings, and nuptial couches.

When the spider is spinning, a close-up of her soft, round abdomen reveals an extraordinary sight. Each spinneret is tipped with a number of fingerlike spinning tubes. And they move like fingers—sorting strands, weaving, twisting them into the appropriate cables with the finger speed of a classical guitarist.

Between the front pair of spinnerets in some spiders is a hairy little appendage called a *colulus*. Nobody yet has figured out what it's for.

The cables make up as many different kinds of webs as there are species of spiders (some forty thousand of them), for no two species make webs identically. All webs are constructed generally in the same way, though; the spider makes a framework, then gradually fills it in.

That little Ariadna, for example, probably built most of her web at night. From the looks of the structure, I was able to reconstruct her major steps fairly accurately, I think. First, she selected the spot—a good one, it turned out, protected from the wind, sheltered somewhat from rain by overhead trees, yet with the main net rather in the open, or at least far enough from the rock to cross insects' flight paths. The funnel-neck retreat hole would be well sheltered underneath the slab. Back through the door at the end of her lair, the spider could find moisture—just in case the summer would be dry. Incidentally, the threat of desiccation isn't so great as with most cryptozoa. Spiders (as well as some flies) have a film of wax in the outermost layer of their exoskeletons. It serves to stop internal water from evaporating.

Ariadna started her web by climbing the oak seedling, crawling out on a twig, and dropping halfway to the ground. Then she simply hung there on her thread, waiting.

Eventually a breeze came up, and soon the wind wafted her to the top of the rock. She caught hold, glued fast the end of the strand, then pulled it tight and glued it again.

She crawled up this bridge, then dropped down again from the same attachment point. And waited. Soon she was blown toward the rock again, but this time she let herself land on the ground just in front of it. Then she climbed back up the strand, transferred to the other, sped down its slant almost to the end, then dropped off, down to strand number two. And that made a three-string triangle.

Then she clambered over to the milkweed plant and ran through the same process.

She then probably attached the two triangles, making a crude sort of funnel of strong scaffolding strands. From that point she simply filled in the open spaces, placing runways for herself here and there, carefully attaching sticky strands for bug trapping in appropriate places, filling in the central orb, lining her retreat hole with long, slender, silken strands, and adding a soft, cottony collar peculiar to her species.

When she was done she had a combination home and trap exceedingly strong, yet very light. Were the structure to be made of strands of steel of the same size, it would be not only heavier, but weaker.

The strands are so uniform in thickness and are so unaffected by temperature and humidity that technicians use them as cross hairs in measuring devices and telescope sights.

How do you get a spider to give you her thread? You take it from her. Professional spider raisers collect strands first by immobilizing the animal—usually with a large staple encircling her narrow waist and stuck into a piece of soft wood—then by tickling her spinnerets with a tiny watercolor paint brush. Quickly she produces a bit of web. The "silker" draws it out and winds it on a wire frame for shipment. Females are the only spiders used. They produce stronger, better quality silk, and much more of it. They can be silked a couple of dozen times (with a few days rest between), each time producing one hundred feet or so of line. Certain Aranea spiders have provided a thousand feet of web in a single strand.

A spider in the wild begins her life as an egg, along with dozens or hundreds (depending on species) of other eggs, crowded into a silken cocoon. The cocoon—usually a beautifully woven, glittering basket—may be tucked away in a corner or under a rock or carried around by mama.

Hatching time, and the first born finds herself without a morsel to eat. Never mind. Wait, and soon another egg hatches, and the newborn brother or sister provides an instant meal. Other spiderlings emerge, and they may or may not be eaten. Eventually, somebody stops the carnage by breaking through the cocoon, freeing everyone.

Once free of the cocoon, some kinds of spiderlings crawl up and cling to the backs of their mothers. Others spend their early days in a sort of webby nursery, while still others live on the main web with mother, feeding on scraps and old carcasses.

In most species, though, a young spider's biggest need is to get away from his brothers and sisters—and parents —to guard against being eaten. The quickest way is by aerial balloon. The baby climbs to the top of a plant, turns to face the wind, lifts her abdomen and spews forth a light, silken strand two or three feet long into the wind. Soon the breeze lifts her into the air, and she balloons away, dangling, guiding herself somewhat by hauling in the line and letting it out again to billow like a spinnaker. Every so often she runs into a tree. She snips off the thread, runs around to the other side, and launches herself again with a new strand.

When the young spider finally lands on an appealing homesite, she weaves her first web—often youthfully sloppy, but in the family tradition. As she grows, she molts, shedding her exoskeleton up to a dozen times before reaching full adulthood. As shedding time approaches, the spider actually digests the inside layer of her skin, and what is left is thin and easily ripped. The new skin pushes outward under the pressure of the blood, and soon the old layer splits near the animal's front, continuing to rip off backwards. She, meantime, is gyrating with pumping motions, doing a slow shimmy. The used exoskeleton—now old and stiff—continues to rip and slide off the flexible new skin. If the spider has lost a leg, often a new one, smaller and weaker, will show itself during the molt.

When females reach adulthood they are almost always larger than males. And the difference in size is of considerable importance to spiders, mainly because most are cannabalistic, and usually it's the male who is eaten.

Poor fellow, he can't always tell if a prospective mate is eager to meet him for his capacity as a lover or (literally) provider. Sometimes both, in the obvious sequence. She won't need him again anyway—at least for some time. A single fertilization may be good for a year or more.

Actually, females don't eat their mates as often as legend would lead one to believe. But males very often die after the exertion of mating. Females, on the other hand, may live several years. Most spiders last only eight or nine months, but some females of the suborder Orthognatha (which includes American tarantulas, trap-doors, and funnelwebs) may live up to twenty years.

At least one spider circumvents the being-eaten problem by brawn. The crab spider—so called because he holds his legs to the side and sidles sideways and backwards like a crab—sneaks up on his prospective mate, lassoes her, then quickly loops threads around her body until she can hardly move. When he has staked her to the ground, he mates with her in safety and at his leisure.

What other kinds of spiders might you find under rocks? Of the forty thousand species that have been named so far—and that's only about a third of the total, most arachnidophiles feel—here is a handful of some of those you might run across:

The House Spider (or Cobweb Weaver or Comb-footed Spider) belongs to the family Theridiidae. This is the family (with more than two hundred American species) usually responsible for those webs up in the corner of the dining room. The members also like to live in the shelter of overhanging rocks. The house-spider web isn't very tidy, but sprawls all over the place. Females can lay nearly two thousand eggs in a single season, but the mortality rate balances out; the spiderlings feed on each other through the first five molts, before leaving the cocoon.

Southern House Spiders (family Filistatidae) are similar in habits to the regular house spiders. They're found in houses as well as under rocks in fields, and they, too, build sloppy webs. Some of the threads are remarkable, however; they stretch to fify times their original lengths.

Though some fifty species are common, not very much is known about any of them. They seem to adapt themselves to life in a terrarium, so if anyone wants to do some original research, here is a good group to start with. They live primarily in the South.

Domestic Platform Spiders or Funnel Weavers (family Agelenidae)—some fifty species of which are found in the U.S.—are quite often seen under rocks. Look for their funnel webs along the bottom of old stone walls when morning dew makes them conspicuous. Call the spider out by tossing a small insect near the perimeter of the web.

In fall, the female dies after forming a disc-shaped egg sac, often while still clinging to it. The female of some species (*Coelotes terrestris,* for instance) shares meals with the young, summoning them by jiggling the web. She even provides her newborn of the following spring with their first meal: herself.

Wolf Spiders (family Lycosidae) are found all over the U.S., but mostly in warmer parts. They're heavy, solid spiders, often more than an inch long. They commonly burrow under rocks and wait in their lair, watching with sharp eyes, rushing out to pounce on their prey in true wolflike fashion.

The female attaches her egg case—containing some two hundred eggs—to her underside and carries it until hatched several weeks later. Some researchers report she will fight to the death to protect the case. Sometimes she loses it, and if she doesn't find it she'll substitute a twig, a bit of paper, a leaf.

The spiderlings ride on her back, climbing up her legs if they fall off—which they do often, as she hunts, pounces, and wrestles with victims. Soon they tire of falling and climbing, and set off on their own.

Adults can be caught by inserting a straw into their burrows and hauling them out like fish. Wolf spiders make excellent pets.

If spiders as a whole have been given a bad press, Tarantulas positively have been libeled. The truth is that the American tarantula of the Southwest is cowardly, is blind or nearly so, and won't bite unless hurt. Further, the bite isn't serious. The fact is, the tarantula's temper is excellent, and he's easily tamed. And that is why among spider buffs the tarantula is a favorite pet.

The reason for the slanderous tales is the belief of people in medieval times that the tarantula of southern Europe (*Lycosa tarentula*) is highly poisonous. It isn't. A further belief is that a bite could cause a disease similar to St. Vitus's dance called "tarantism." The only way to rid oneself of the disease, so the old wives said, was by dancing. Some historians believe that the dance was a cover for certain heathen rites outlawed by Christians. At any rate, our tarantula had nothing to do with it.

The Black Widow is the world's most famous spider, and it's just about the only one most people can identify—because of that bright red hourglass on a black body. Unfortunately, the marking isn't always an hourglass; it may be a red splotch or spot, or even yellow. And doubly unfortunate, a widow needn't even be black. The Brown Widow (*Latrodectus geometricus*) is a brownish-gray, and the Red Widow (*L. bishopi*) is orange. Both these Florida residents are poisonous, but less so than the black variety (*L. mactans*). Only the females of any of them, however, are potent. The males, only half as large as the females, neither bite nor even feed, but spend their short lives wandering glumly in search of females.

Mostly found in warmer climates, black widows have been known to live in every state but Alaska and Hawaii. They stay outside, usually, near shelters—in dumps, in stone walls, and under rocks, where a spider might bite a hand carelessly thrust. The widow's web is funnel-shaped, but not very well done. She hangs feet upward, waiting —often for her succulent mate, satisfying in at least two respects.

How bad is the bite? Says Willis John Gertsch, former Curator of Spiders at the American Museum of Natural History in New York: "The black widow is probably the most poisonous among all venomous creatures, [with poison] fifteen times as potent as rattlesnake venom." At first a bite may be unnoticed, but the subsequent pains—in the abdomen, soles of the feet, eyelids—may be severe, and the patient may be in for several days of agony. Medication helps. However, I cannot find a verified record of a healthy adult human being having died as a result of a black widow bite—though some sixty bites a year are recorded in the U.S.—mainly because the spider doesn't carry much poison with her.

The Brown Recluse or Fiddler (*Loxesceles reclusus*) is a half-inch, oval-bodied spider that only recently was found to be poisonous. But dangerous it is, particularly so because in appearance it seems insignificant. Chocolate or fawn-colored, its distinguishing mark is a violin-shaped blotch on its head, but this is often difficult to see.

The recluse seeks the dark—in crevices, in barns, in stone walls, under rocks, and, unfortunately, in shoes and bed-clothes. And that's the problem. Though the spider is really shy and mild-mannered, when squashed by a toe or rolling body he reacts and chomps down on the offender.

When he does, the venom may cause only a mosquito-bite sting, but a few hours later the wound develops into white agony, accompanied by joint pains, cramps, and fever. The bitten area may grow gangrenous, requiring it to be excised, perhaps even necessitating a skin graft to close the hole that's left.

Presently the brown recluse ranges from Texas to Wisconsin and from the Carolinas to Colorado. It seems to be spreading northward.

Daddy-Longlegs or Harvestmen (order Phalangida) aren't really spiders at all—though they are arachnids. The difference between the two is in the attachment of the cephalothorax to the abdomen. In spiders the two lobes are well defined, connected by a narrow stalk. In harvest-men (and scorpions and mites, other arachnids), the attachment is broad, so thick it sometimes isn't discernible. On first glance a harvestman's body seems to be oval as a pill. But a closer look reveals it to be an overweight dumb-bell.

Also, spiders usually have eight eyes. Harvestmen—at least in the one hundred to two hundred American species —have two.

Female daddy-longlegs (mamma-longlegs?) use long, stout ovipositors to thrust eggs into the ground in the fall. The young emerge the following spring to live a year or two. They feed on dead insects and other animals, on plant juices, and sometimes on living insects.

Beetles—the most varied insect—make up what has been called the most successful order of animals in the world. More than a quarter-million different kinds crawl the earth (26,500 have been recorded in the U.S.), making up about 40 percent of all insects. They range in size from a 1/100-inch fungus beetle to the four-and-a-half inch, banana-peeling Goliath and the half-foot *Dynastes hercules* beetles. Some fly, some swim, some walk—and a good variety live under rocks, swarming out of the cryptosphere only in the humid air of night.

Capture something that *looks* like a beetle and it usually is. But to make sure, check the wings, the mouth, and if possible, the life history.

A beetle has four wings, but only the back two are used in flying. The front pair, called *elytra* (pronounced el'-ee-tra, singular elytron)—thickened and stiff—are used to protect the back pair. They're folded back over the thin, fragile flying wings, neat. When flying, the beetle lifts his elytra and holds them high out of the way while his hind-wings whirr him along. The arrangement gives the beetle his order name: Coleoptera, which means "sheath-wings." A few beetles have lost their functional wings, however, and in these the elytra may be fused along the back.

The mouth of a beetle is primitive, designed for chewing

solids. More highly developed orders have mouths that are specialized—for lapping with a spongy tongue (houseflies), for instance, or for sipping nectar and sap (butterflies, mosquitoes). Beetles must tear off and chew their food.

As for life history, beetles go through a complete metamorphosis, progressing through four distinct stages—egg, larva, pupa, adult—usually living in separate places and eating different foods. Many newly hatched insects—grasshoppers and aphids, for example—are tiny versions of the adult. Not so with beetles. The caterpillarlike larva has no resemblance whatever to what it will become.

The skin of a larva doesn't stretch, so as the insect grows it must discard the old to reveal the new, slightly larger, suit. Most beetle larvae molt a half-dozen or more times —until they are larger than adult size—before going into the pupa stage. Beetle larvae, by the way, are known as grubs; those of the fly, maggots; of the butterfly and moth, caterpillars.

During its drastic change from a crawling creature to a flying adult, a beetle pupa eats nothing, moves little (except for an energetic tail waggle if picked up), and is virtually helpless. His only protection is his tough skin, plus the rock or soil that covers him. This stage may last a few days, weeks, or months. Then the skin splits and the adult emerges—humping, straining, struggling up through the split, then laboriously pulling his head and legs free. Usually the newly-emerged adult is pale and gaunt, but his full color ordinarily develops in a few hours.

That adult is a remarkable creature. For one thing, he is one of the world's strongest. Some beetles can support weights more than eight hundred times their own. If human beings could do the same, an average man could carry the entire National Football League on his back.

The ears of many beetles possess a double range of hearing. One scale is tuned to the cries of other beetles—particularly the sound of potential mates. The other is sensitive to the sounds made by bats. If a flying beetle hears an approaching bat he may simply tuck his wings close and plummet to earth—hopefully before the bat detects him.

When frightened or attacked, some beetles retaliate with a foul-smelling spray. Best known of these is the *Brachinus* or Bombardier Beetle, a half-inch, night-roaming insect that spends his days hidden under rocks. When disturbed he clobbers his enemy by squeezing himself and squirting fine repellent streams, like a pin-pricked garden hose. Each squirt is accompanied by an audible "pop," a miniature explosion.

In 1969 entomologists discovered that the beetle's spray isn't only highly noxious, but scalding as well. Four men from Cornell University, working with a particular bombardier species with shiny, sky-blue wings and head and trunk of glowing orange, noticed that whenever they handled the beasts they felt a burning sensation—almost as though they were being squirted with boiling water. To check the temperature they arranged things so that agitated beetles discharged on a sensitive thermometer.

The temperature: 212° F. The substance, they found after a good deal of chemical sleuthing, is quinone, which is made (in case anyone cares) by rapidly bringing together a mixture of hydroquinones and hydrogen peroxide with certain enzymes. They react so strongly, the mixture instantly boils, propelling out the caustic fluid. Each beetle is able to blast a number of times before he must rest. One, in fact, sprayed twenty-nine ejections in a row before exhaustion.

What other beetles might a beetle buff find hiding beneath rocks? Thousands of kinds, actually, but here is a sampling of some of the possibilities.

Swift-running Ground Beetles (family Carabidae), a whole variety of them (2,200 in the U.S., someone estimated), are likely candidates to be found under rocks. Usually they're about an inch long and black or brown—but not always. They prefer rocks in rather moist areas. Active mostly at night, they run down and devour such prey as caterpillars and other slow-moving insects.

The Horned Passalus (*Passalus cornutus*) is easily identifiable by a hook atop his head, bent forward. The fascinating thing about this fellow is that he is one of the very few species of beetles that (1) is communal, and (2) can make sounds. The noise is a chirpy squeak, and it's produced when passalus rubs the corrugated lower surface of his wing covers against certain hard projections on the upper surface of his abdomen. The sound probably serves to keep the colony together—stopping both grubs and adults from wandering off.

Horned passaluses are found in rotting logs and under rocks in mulchy areas, usually in hardwood forests.

Click Beetles, of the seven hundred–member Elateridae family, are fascinating little creatures found all across the United States. The name (in some sections they're called "skipjacks") comes from the beetle's method of righting himself when somehow he finds himself on his back. Which happens often, because it is his custom to roll up in a ball, folding his legs tight, when frightened. And if he happens to be on a plant, he plummets to the ground.

Likely as not he lands on his back. He waits a few moments for the danger to pass, then bends himself backward in the middle, pulling tight a springlike spine on his chest. Suddenly he lets go, the built-up tension is released, and his forepart snaps straight. The action jerks him into the air four inches or so with an audible snap. If he lands on his back again he immediately pops up—and he'll keep on popping until finally he lands on his legs and scurries off under a rock, away from his pursuers.

He also uses the trick if he finds himself entrapped in a bird's bill or a boy's palm. And the result usually is the same: instant freedom.

Carrion or Burying Beetles (*Necrophorus marginatus,* for example) of the Silphidae family, spend their leisure time under rocks, but are best known for their activity around dead animals. When an animal dies, carrion beetles sniff it out, home in with a flight pattern of constricting circles, antennae stretched forward like—well, antennae. They land on or near the animal, and carefully walk around it, examining and considering possibilities like civil engineers planning a project. They usually bother with the corpse only if it is rat-size or smaller.

If the ground is sandy or soft, they leave the animal where it is; if hard or rocky, they drag it, in a remarkable display of teamwork, to a suitable spot. Then they dig around and around the body, excavating a grave so the animal sinks lower and lower until the top is about on a level with the surface. Then they deposit eggs on the body and flick dirt over it until buried. The young will be born surrounded by dinner.

In two or three hours (for a mouse) to perhaps six or seven (for a squirrel), no evidence remains but a freshly-turned plot of soil. The beetles must work fast, for if flies get there before the animal is covered, the corpse might be consumed by maggots long before the beetle babies ever hatch.

All of the dozen American species of *Necrophorus* are between one and two inches long, rather stubby and black, usually with a spot or two of red on each elytron. A few species grow golden hair on their thorax. Usually the forewings don't reach all the way back to cover the abdomen.

Incidentally, beetle collectors sometimes place meat out for bait, then cover it with an overturned box so neighborhood dogs don't run off with it. With luck, a whole army of carrion beetles will be attracted as the meat gets ripe.

Ant Beetles, other members of the Silphidae family, are sometimes found leisurely living in red ant nests, and pose an interesting philosophical problem to entomologists. The ants apparently seek the beetles out, provide them with a home, clean them, give them food, dote on them. How come? "Perhaps they're tolerated by the ants because of the good they do in cleaning up waste material in the nest," suggests one authority. Another eminent entomologist offers the suggestion that "they probably are kept because of their exciting aroma," and adds, "I'd classify them as symbiotic parasites."

But other biologists are unsatisfied with these explanations. Yet the alternatives seem equally unacceptable. Listen to Thomas Carroll, biologist with New York's Rondout Valley School System: "The ants actually go out and find these beetles, these seemingly *attractive* beetles, and they keep them in underground rooms with doors too small for them to escape. Biologists refuse to use the obvious word, *pet,* and they're going out of their heads trying to figure out what it all means."

8. Three Communes

In the fall of 1931, so I was told, a couple of kids wandering through the woods came to a dead pine halfway up that New York hillside. It had stood there, dead, for nearly a dozen years, and most of its limbs had fallen off. During the first few years, fungus ate at its innards, beetles bored through it, and woodpeckers, following the insects, burrowed into its interior. But gradually the pine hardened, as woods often do when dry. The process of decay, of disintegration, slowed.

Then the boys came along—and human beings, after all, are also part of Earth's ecosystems. They pushed the tree over. It struck the rock and broke at the impact point. All winter, snows covered the broken trunk, and by the time the spring sun had driven the snow away, the tree was water-soaked and punky.

During the morning of April 24, 1932, it rained. In mid-afternoon, at a spot some three hundred feet from the rock, a strange event took place. From a BB-size hole in the ground, half-inch insects streamed. They looked a

An enlarged view of an ant commune. (The queen ant isn't shown.)

little like ants, with brownish-black bodies and two identical pairs of long, gossamer, whitish wings. But they were paler than ants, and they had thick, rather than wasplike waists. They were would-be kings and queens of *Reticulitermes flanipes*. Termites.

They oozed up out of the ground by the hundreds, each hesitating before the exit door—thunderstruck by the harsh light—then were bumped out into the open by those pushing behind. One by one they set off on the only flight they'd ever take, one they had been preparing for all winter—all their lives, in fact.

They flew slowly and cumbersomely, scattering in all directions—to the utter delight of birds, salamanders, spiders, and toads anxious for a banquet.

Most of the termites that made it through the hungry hordes weren't much better off than those that didn't. They landed on lakes or streams or roads or some other inhospitable place, and sooner or later died. Many that did manage to set down in an ideal place couldn't find anyone to share it with, and their lives were wasted, too. Of the hundreds of termites that swarmed out of that hole, perhaps only two became founders of a new nest.

One of those—a queen—landed near the New York rock, next to the spot where the tree lay against the ground, decomposing. She tried to walk through the grass, but her wings were in the way. So she forced them back, so far they cracked off at a suture at their base like a piece of tablet paper along a perforated line.

Once rid of her wings she stuck her abdomen high in the air, squeezed something inside her, and flatulated, wafting a touch of gas enormously attractive to male termites. One who happened to be sailing about the sky sniffing for just such a scent came plumping down beside her, and she trotted off with him behind, like a two-car train. They stopped where the log met the ground and together excavated a little chamber just below the surface and sealed themselves off from the world. They never saw daylight again.

In a few weeks the bridal couple became parents of two dozen white nymphs, miniatures of themselves. On these rested the future of the colony, and so they were especially well taken care of, fed with droplets of regurgitated food from the mouths of their parents. Some of the sustenance came from wood eaten by the adults, but most was adsorbed and reused wing muscle, no longer useful.

The royal couple passed on something else, too, equally as important: certain intestinal protozoa consisting of a special group of *flagellates,* single-cell organisms with whipping tails. Such protozoa are absolutely necessary, for a termite cannot digest his own food; the flagellates, living in the alimentary canal, change the cellulose of wood into sugars and other usable materials. Termites simply provide the raw material for them both. Neither organism can live alone.

Termites aren't born with the protozoa. They must get them from others in the colony. Moreover, every time a termite grows large enough to molt it loses not only its skin but also the lining and contents of its stomach, and it must acquire a new set of flagellates from its friends. And that's one reason why termites live in communes; none could live alone. Interestingly, though some three hundred kinds of termite flagellates have been identified, only one or two species are found in any single termite colony. And protozoa from one colony may be utterly worthless in the stomachs of termites on the other side of the hill.

Just as the adsorbed muscles of the new king and queen were about used up, the young had grown enough to find food for themselves—from that decaying log—and to feed their parents as well. They also began to enlarge the chamber, dig new tunnels, take care of the eggs, and everything else that needed to be done around the colony except lay eggs and fertilize the queen, which the king took care of from time to time.

The queen became fatter and fatter as her ovaries grew until she was nothing more than an egg-laying machine, sprawling in her royal chamber with the king, laying thousands of eggs a day, day after day, summer, winter, year after year. (Tropical termite queens, big as frankfurters, can lay seven thousand eggs a day or more, and along with the king can live up to fifty years.)

The young laborers in this new colony belonged to the worker caste. Like bees and ants, the termite society is based on the caste system. But unlike bees and ants, termite workers (and soldiers, the other main caste) include both male and female insects. Ordinarily, they don't reproduce, but can if they need to—if the termite queen or king is killed, for instance. They wouldn't be so good at egg laying, but their large numbers would compensate for inefficiency.

Actually, the resemblance of termites to bees and ants is superficial. The nearest relative to the termite is the cockroach, which is perhaps the oldest insect in the world. The termite and roach probably evolved from a common ancestor.

During those first few weeks of the life of the new colony only a single soldier developed out of the dozen or so young. Nature takes a gamble that a new colony won't be attacked, that it's best to get things humming rather than invest in armament insurance. So only one grotesque, terrible-jawed soldier appeared—wingless, blind, white, and nearly eyeless, as are all nonroyal termites. Hardheaded, too. Soldiers bang their heads against the tunnel sides when disturbed to spread alarm. (If those two boys had returned, rapped on the log, then put their ears against it, they could have heard the vibration alarm.)

The jaws of the soldier were so enormous the young insect couldn't feed himself, so as is always the case, the workers had to shove food down his throat. If ants did attack (ants are termites' principal enemy) and try to gain entrance to the nest, the soldier first would try to block the opening with his head, then would fight the enemy off as the workers walled him off from the colony—a sacrificed martyr.

But in this case no such sacrifice was necessary. And in the meantime, the workers—looking pretty much like the soldier except for his awful mouth—were enlarging the house. They dug down into the earth to assure themselves of a constant moisture supply, and they chomped long, convoluted tunnels into the log. They even built a short-cut tunnel to get from the log down the side of the rock into the earth—a tunnel, because they disdain light so much they must carry their darkness and moist atmosphere with them. If removed from the snug coziness of their tunnels for a few hours, in fact, they die.

For tunnel material they used excrement mixed with particles of soil to make fast-setting and waterproof cement. They constructed the passageway in a curious and seemingly inefficient manner. A worker knocked a tiny hole in the end of the tunnel, no bigger than his head, then quickly plugged it again, a little farther out, with a particle of soil mixed with cement. Then he knocked out an adjacent piece and plugged *that* opening out a ways farther, while other workers butted and recemented alongside. Gradually, with the destruction and addition of millions of particles, the tube stretched up the rock. The whole bridge was completed in only two round-the-clock days of work.

About a year after the colony was established another class of citizens appeared: the "secondary royal" caste. They were young males and females, darker than the others in the colony, with wings. These were the hope-fully-to-be kings and queens of new colonies. One warm spring day after a rain, a worker kicked a hole in the tunnel running up the side of the rock, and one by one the young-sters blundered their way into the daylight and flew off. As the last one stumbled out the door, a worker jammed a clod of dirt into the tunnel hole, shutting out the awful light.

Not quite all the young royalty left the colony. A few individuals, sexually mature but blind and nearly wingless, stayed with their fellows. These were the substitute roy-alty chosen to ascend the throne in case one of the reigning pair died. (In some cases, these "secondary reproduc-tives," as they sometimes are called, are allowed to lay a small but continuing number of eggs, and among some termite species the total number of eggs layed by a large number of substitute royalty surpasses the number layed by the queen.)

As the years fluttered past, the pine gradually settled down into the ground, worked on by bacteria, fungi, in-sects, and the termites. In a decade virtually nothing of it could be seen, and the rain gradually washed away the dung-colored tunnel running up the side of the rock.

Meantime, an oak, some thirty feet up the hill, died, and gradually *it* became the prime source of food as the hundreds of thousands of termites slowly migrated in that direction, continuing in their essential work of converting wood to soil.

Today that original colony is still going strong about a thousand feet up the gully. And the workers have found a great new source of dead pine. People, it seems, have built houses of it.

Before, during, and after the era of the termites, ants, large and small, red and black, mean and placid, crawled under, on, and around the rock. One kind or another established itself shortly after the slab was deposited on the hillside, and some kind or other has been around ever since—for eighteen thousand years, more or less, when the ice sheet finally left. They like living under the rock because it grows warm in the noonday sun and holds the heat through the night. It protects and hides them, too, with no chance of a cave-in.

At one time small, dark brown Cornfield Ants (*Lasius niger*) used the rock for shelter as they went about their curious habit of cultivating aphids for the sweet honeydew they exude. Each fall the ants carried the succulent insects down into the ground to hibernate at the roots of grasses, and each spring they gathered them up again and toted them onto plants to feed. And during the summers they fussed over them like they were prize dairy cows—which, more or less, they were.

During another period Black Honey Ants (*Camponotus inflatus*) called the rock home. They get their name because of the offbeat way they store food in bountiful times.

Some of the ants, called "repletes," become living storage vats. Food gatherers lap up sweet excretion from oak galls and aphids, carry it home, then regurgitate it and pump it into the repletes' mouths. In their innards it's transformed into honey. Then they store it in their ballooning abdomens. When food is scarce, the storage tanks are available to anyone who wants a meal.

During still another period the slavemaking Sanguinary Ants (*Formica sanguinea*) used the rock's underside as a base for their operations. These 3/8-inch, dull red creatures raid other colonies—often of ants bigger than themselves—fighting their way to the brood chambers and carrying off larvae and pupae. Back home they tend the alien young with the utmost love and affection—for when they grow up, the captives work as energetically as though they were back in their original colony, taking over the bulk of the labor in the nest.

No matter what the variety, however, and whether they numbered from only a few members to several hundred thousand, all the ants who lived under the rock ran their societies by the same general rules. They all were made up of three castes, for instance: queens, males, and workers, highly specialized for an amazing variety of jobs.

The queen, after founding a new colony (in a manner strikingly similar to the queen termite—but without a king), becomes a corpulent egg-laying blob. She usually is unable to feed or care for herself, and often is barely able to move; to do so, she often must be shoved or virtually carried by her aides. Ordinarily only one queen reigns. Toward the latter part of her decade-long life, however, when her egg production is slowing, auxiliary queens begin to grow in the colony. They all live there together in peace and harmony—a situation, incidentally, never tolerated in a bee hive. There, the queen stings to death any potential ruler while it is still in its pupation cell.

The males (*not* called "kings" in the world of ants) are useful only during the marriage flight. When the big day comes for the young, almost-queen *termite* and her king-to-be to fly off for the honeymoon, they are reluctant to leave the snug darkness of their nest. Not so with ants. Excited by sex and an urge to stretch their wings, they must be held back by the workers until the time is just right. Just what makes it right is something the ants know and we don't, but somehow they all know together, because all at once—usually toward evening—from all the colonies from miles around would-be queens and consorts blossom up at roughly the same time, almost by prearrangement. Good thing, too—otherwise there would be too much intracolony breeding.

This is the first and last flight of their lives. But unlike the young termites, the ants mate in flight, the male depositing enough sperm for millions of future ants. He puts it in her purselike *spermatheca,* from which she will draw for the rest of her life.

The male, spent but happy, flies off. He'll flit about for a few days—perhaps a couple of weeks—then curl up and die, his job well done.

The queen, though, after rubbing off her wings on a log or stone, digs a little room in the soil, seals herself in, and starts her family. She feeds the larvae with her mouth, using a secretion she manufactures from her excess fat and wing muscles. Slowly the pupae, isolated in their self-spun cocoons, develop into adults who can feed mamma. It's a long wait for her, though, sometimes a number of months —with some species ten or more. And all the time she hasn't had a single bite of food.

The workers, sterile females, finally appear. They're little, stunted things, these first ones, called *minims,* and they aren't very effective as workers go. But by this time the queen is glad to see *anyone.* The minims kick open a door to the sunlight and tromp out looking for food—anything, at this point, from dead animals to living insects to old dried carcasses to dung. They hurry back to the queen with their mouthfuls, and from then on her worries are over—just so long as her ovaries keep on pumping out eggs.

The next batch of young are normal-sized workers, able to do an honest day's job. Some act as excavators, some as nursemaids, some as housekeepers. Others are hunters and food gatherers (an ordinary ant can lift the equivalent of a man hoisting four tons), shepherds (or aphisherds), or simply explorers, trotting about with haste when the air is warm, more slowly when chilly. (One Harvard researcher found that he could measure air temperature within 1° F. by timing the speed of a walking ant. At 100° F., he reported in the Proceedings of the National Academy of Sciences, they move fifteen times faster than they do at 50°.)

Other workers are soldiers. Some of them truly were born for duty, for they have huge heads—sometimes used to plug entranceways—and dragonlike jaws. Most soldiers, however, seem to be conscripts drafted for the job as crises arise. According to at least one entomologist/writer, Peter Farb, the "soldier sentinels" posted in hours-long shifts at various apparently vulnerable spots around a colony aren't really soldiering at all. Though they have the characteristic soldier stance of close-drawn legs, bodies hunched against the ground, and laid-back antennae, they're really loafing. They're "exhibiting a little-known characteristic of ants—their laziness," writes Farb. "These loafing and probably rather timid ants . . . serve the nest simply by being dispersed widely. . . . If foreign ants invade, the action may excite some solitary loafer enough to arouse the rest of the community."

One function where there is no faking work, however, is in excavation. The structure of an ant house is amazing. The center of activity is the underside of the rock, under which is located the sun-warmed nursery. Downstairs from the solarium are dozens of stories, each with rooms, chambers, corridors, and halls supported by intricately-placed pillars and shafts. If some solidifying liquid could be poured in and the earth washed away, the result might look something like a car-size sponge.

The young are reared near the underside of the rock because that's often the warmest spot in the house. Unfortunately, the room temperatures near the surface are always changing—hot during the day, but cold at night. So the nursemaids are forever carrying the young upstairs and down, laying them in heaps in different rooms. As the Englishman John Crompton puts it in his *Ways of the Ant,* "It is as if we carried a naked baby about the house into whatever room was being warmed by the sun; then at night down into the kitchen." Bears, incidentally, turn over rocks to find ants and their young. Such nocturnal animals as raccoons and skunks, however, who might also enjoy an ant meal, lose out. When *they're* awake the ants are far underground.

In theory an ant colony, like a city, is a perpetual thing. Queens of most species live for a dozen years or so, and when one dies the colony is prepared—newly developed queens are waiting in the wings. The homefolks send out thousands of youngsters for mating, trusting that at least one will happen to plop back fully fertilized, near the nest. Fortunately, this usually happens. Sometimes not. And if it doesn't, the commune may wither and die.

Three summers ago a chipmunk burrowed a backdoor passage under the rock. For some reason the corridor wasn't very satisfactory, because as soon as autumn approached, he abandoned it. The hole wasn't wasted, though. Next spring a queen Yellow Jacket (*Vespula maculifrons*) found it and established a colony, and the burrow was enlarged eventually to hold a pumpkin-size city of ten thousand before the hints of impending disaster first appeared.

The saga of the city of yellow jackets actually started the previous fall when the virgin queen set off on her maiden flight. She was a lovely thing, really, with yellow- and black-colored hairs waving in complex, exquisitely detailed patterns over her body. Somewhere up in the blue she romped about, and fell to earth a virgin no longer. Came the cold, she crawled away to some protected place —possibly under a sliver of a hickory's shagbark—and slept through the winter.

In the spring she went house hunting, and during her rounds happened on the chipmunk burrow under the rock. She poked her head down the opening, then flew off to find possibly a better spot, returned to the rock, buzzed into the hole, flew off again, then returned for good. Here she would start her city.

She selected a rather level section of the tunnel, then laboriously rolled stones out of the way to make a flat clearing. Repeatedly she flew to a splintery log down the hillside, there to rip off bits of wood to mix with her saliva to form construction material. She erected pillars and walls, then covered them with a broad canopy, cementing it firmly against the burrow ceiling, using plant roots poking through the roof for anchors and guy wires. Onto her paper ceiling she constructed a dozen tiny, hexagonal cups or cells, the *comb* opening downward. And into each she laid an egg, cementing it into place so it wouldn't fall out.

In the eight days before the eggs hatched, she kept busy by sealing off the burrow that the chipmunk had used, and beginning work on the second story of the city—*below* the first. Grain by grain she dug the earth away until she had enough room. Then she began building a hanging floor, attached to the pillars that at first seemed to *support* the roof. But before she could construct very much her brood hatched—chubby, soft-bodied grubs stuck onto the tops of the cells by a sticky disk at the rear end of their bodies.

Older wasps live mainly on nectar, but youngsters need raw meat. So the queen flew out and attacked small insects, partially digesting them. Back in the nursery the infants were acting like baby birds, mouths agape. Others were asleep. The queen, swollen with minced fly, approached one sleeping grub and poked it with her antenna. It awakened and nodded about, swinging its blind head, trying to feel the food. She stuck her mouthparts into its and transferred a droplet of food. The grub went back to sleep.

In another week or so the larvae had grown as large as their cells. Each spun a veil around itself and attached the hood to the cell's top, then continued spinning until it had enclosed its head and shoulders in a bag. Another several days and they emerged as full-fledged wasps eager to take up the various duties of a hive and to leave the exhausted mother to do what she does best—lay eggs.

The queen's nursing duties were taken over by a pro, one of the newly hatched adults. The new nurse efficiently strode along the corridors giving sips to this one and that, touching one, stroking another, helping a third to adjust his position. Occasionally one of the youngsters would be puny, not developing as fast as she thought it should—and then she gave a hint of the true nature of wasps, and of the coming catastrophe. She would approach the sickly baby, grab it by the scruff of the neck, haul it from the cell, drag it to the edge of the comb and hurl it off. It would land in a large, scooped out area below the nest that had become a trash heap, the town dump. For awhile it would lie there wiggling. Finally it would die.

Meanwhile, the queen increased her laying rate—by the score, then hundreds, then thousands.

Elsewhere, most of the work went into constructing the city. For material the builders used a few plant stems, but mostly rotting slivers of fallen trees and pieces of old, weather-worn fences yanked off with their jaws. They converted the raw material to gray papier-mâché siding by chewing it well with saliva. Then they'd spit out a mouthful of pulpy mash, form it into a slip of paper, and using jaws and feet as tools, join it to the edge of the sheet, patting it and smoothing it nicely in place.

The earth in the city's cellar was scooped away by thousands and thousands of wasps to make way for the growing hive. Each granule was carried out of the entrance and far away so predators wouldn't notice the hole. (Strange as it seems some animals like to eat yellow jackets. One hunter who examined the stomach of an American black bear found two quarts of them, swallowed whole.)

The floors of the city were extended sideways and additional stories were added to the bottom. As different sources of wood were used, bands appeared on the nest walls—different colors of gray and brown. Walls were made in layers upon layers. If a wall were a single, continuous sheet it would give little protection against the cold. But constructed in blanketlike layers, the stagnant, trapped air acts as insulation. When an overhead comb section became rickety from use, instead of rebuilding it, the insects would abandon it, preferring to construct another wing instead. New flying buttresses appeared, rooms were enlarged, floors renovated. The city was abustle with activity. If somehow an important stranger stumbled into the hole, he was immediately set upon by dozens and dozens of wasps, stung to death if possible, then shoved off the combs onto the rubbish heap.

By the middle of summer a new kind of cell began to grow—huge, bullet-shaped things, a third larger than the others, almost like small peanuts poking from the combs. These held the young royalty, and as the babies grew they were slathered over by the nurses, fed particularly wholesome food, fondled and catered to, cleaned and caressed, and given a story all to themselves.

Suddenly one sunny afternoon in early fall they were gone—loosed by their guardians to fly off on their wedding flight and to found new empires.

After the departure of the princes and princesses, the hive somehow seemed to lose spirit. The building of new sections slowed. The combs started to look used and somewhat frazzled as household duties were relaxed. The queen, weary, layed fewer and fewer eggs, and spent more and more time flopped in a corner. Workers began fighting among themselves, anxious and nervous and imbued with a sense of coming doom. The commune was dispirited, failing, falling apart.

The worst was what was happening in the nursery. The young were hungry, but the nurse fed them only infrequently, then hardly at all. Then she began to pick on them. She poked them and bit them and tortured them. Other workers joined in, and as the barbaric fever spread, more were attracted, then converted. They grasped the grubs and hauled them from their cells, likely as not ripping the flesh in the process. Savagely they dragged them out, glorying in the brutality as one by one the young were destroyed, their bodies, often still pulsating, thrown on the garbage heap. As the insanity seeped through the colony, the workers rushed about destroying, looting, ransacking. Then the queen was assassinated. And then the workers tore open the unhatched eggs and devoured them. Finally they began killing each other, and soon only a relatively few were left—then these, too, began to die. Some crawled out onto the earth's surface, thrashed a bit, then lay still. Most pulled themselves to the edge of the comb, fell into the waste pit on their backs, and moved no more. Oddly, none died on the combs; the code of comb cleanliness remained too strong.

Soon the occasional fluttering of wings or the painful pulsing of abdomens was the only movement in the echoing halls. The long, low-ceilinged chambers grew silent, the inverted cradles lay empty, and the only body left in the nursery was that of the queen, huddled and broken, in the corner.

Even before the last few yellow jackets died, however, other creatures came slinking in to loot. Silverfish and mites, spiders and beetles moved in to lap up any remaining nectar. Mice roamed the corridors, sniffing and munching.

Winter settled in. By next spring all that was left of the wasp city of thousands were a few shreds of gray paper, a smattering of wing fragments, a little dust that hinted of yellow and black.

Appendix: How to Stalk Bugs

Now, hopefully, the reader will want to go out and look under rocks himself. But a practiced bug hunter can spot a multitude of living creatures where a novice can see only dirt and moldered leaves. Here are a few bug-chasing tips from seasoned searchers:

When you turn over a rock, wait. Don't replace it too soon. Some of the tiny creatures may take a minute or more to work up enough courage to move. So sit and stare awhile.

Look at the underside of the rock, too. Someone may be hanging there, hiding.

Take along a magnifying glass—a couple of them, in fact: one with low magnification to study things in place, another with higher power for closer looks.

You might find a white sheet useful, too. Sprinkle earth scraped from under a rock upon it and chances are something will show itself by moving.

Try some night hunting with a flashlight. Sometimes creatures are found under rocks during hours of darkness that are absent during the day. Cover the lens with a piece of red cellophane and you'll not frighten your quarry so readily.

Replace the rock when you leave. This sounds like an insignificant thing to do in this era of strip mining and bulldozing. But it's not; if you leave the rocks tipped over and return a few weeks later you'll probably be disgusted with the way you left the place.

Here's another suggestion: Keep a notebook. Scientists still know only a tiny amount about most creatures, and your observation might help fill the lack. For instance, almost all books say

American chameleons hatch in about six weeks. But a teenager I know kept records that prove the incubation period is only half that. In another case nobody knew whether or not a certain spider constructs a web. It remained a mystery until a high school naturalist discovered that the spider spun one every evening and took it down again each dawn. What might *you* discover? How long land snails live, for instance. Nobody knows for sure.

Further Information

General Biology Background

Burk, Margaret Wing. *In Yards and Gardens*. Abingdon, 1952. (Light look at insects for grades 4–9.)

Farb, Peter. *The Forest*. Time-Life Books, 1963.

———. *The Insects*. Time-Life Books, 1967.

———. *Living Earth*. Harper, 1959.

Goran, Morris. *Experimental Biology for Boys*. Rider, 1961. (Variety of simple experiments to reveal the joy of discovery.)

McCormick, Jack. *The Living Forest*. Harper, 1959.

Milne, Lorus J. and Margery. *The Mating Instinct*. Little, Brown, 1954.

———. *The Senses of Animals and Men*. Atheneum, 1964.

Thompson, Sir D'Arcy. *On Growth and Form*. Cambridge, 1961 (originally 1917). (Highly technical, but fascinating study of the physics of biology.)

Tinbergen, Niko. *Animal Behavior*. Time-Life Books, 1965.

———. *Curious Naturalists*. Doubleday, 1958. (Anecdotal treatment of natural scientists in action.)

Walsh, John, and Gannon, Robert. *Time Is Short and the Water Rises*. Dutton, 1967. (Anecdotal treatment of selected spiders, centipedes, etc., of the South American rain forest.)

Webster, Gary. *Codfish, Cats and Civilization*. Doubleday, 1955. (Offbeat facts and anecdotes about a variety of animals.)

Natural History Encyclopedias

The Audubon Nature Encyclopedia. Curtis, 1965. (12 vols.)
Illustrated Library of the Natural Sciences. Simon and Schuster, 1958. (4 vols.)
New Illustrated Animal Kingdom. Greystone Press, 1961. (16 vols.)

Fieldbooks

Benton, Allen H., and Werner, W. E., Jr. *Field Biology and Ecology.* Burgess, 1961. (Excellent how-to of field techniques.)
Comstock, Anna Botsford. *Handbook of Nature-Study.* Comstock Publishing; Cornell University Press, 1957 (originally 1911).
Howard, Leland. *The Insect Book.* Doubleday, 1904.
Jaques, H. E. *How to Know the Insects.* Wm. C. Brown, 1947.
Lutz, Frank E. *Field Book of Insects.* Putnam's, 1935. (Old reliable.)
Palmer, E. Laurence. *Fieldbook of Natural History.* Whittlesey House, McGraw-Hill, 1949. (My favorite fieldbook.)
Zim, Herbert S. *Insects.* Simon and Schuster, 1956.

Soil Biology

Kevan, D. K. McE., ed. *Soil Zoology.* Butterworth, London, 1955.
Russell, Sir John. *The World of the Soil.* Collins, London, 1957.
Stanier, R. Y., and others. *The Microbial World.* Prentice-Hall, 1957.

Fungi

Christensen, Clyde. *Molds and Man.* University of Minnesota Press, 1951.
Duddington, C. L. *The Friendly Fungi.* Faber & Faber, London, 1957.
Hutchins, Ross E. *Plants Without Leaves.* Dodd, Mead, 1966. (For youngsters age 10 and up.)
Kavaler, Lucy. *The Wonders of Fungi.* Day, 1964.
Large, E. C. *The Advance of the Fungi.* Dover, 1962. (Case histories of technical fungi discoveries.)
Shuttleworth, Floyd S., and Zim, Herbert S. *Non-flowering Plants.* Golden Press, 1967.

Nematodes

Goodney, T. *Soil and Fresh Water Nematodes.* Methuen, London, 1951.

Spiders, Mites, Centipedes, Millipedes

Baker, E. W., and Wharton, G. W. *Introduction to Acarology.* Macmillan, 1952. (Good, if somewhat technical, outline on mites.)

Barnes, R. D. *Invertebrate Zoology.* Saunders, 1968. (Fine text on crustacea, myriopods, and arachnids.)

Cloudsley-Thompson, J. L. *Spiders, Scorpions, Centipedes and Mites.* Pergamon Press, 1958.

Emerton, James H. *The Common Spiders of the United States.* Dover, 1961.

Gertsch, W. J. *American Spiders.* Van Nostrand, 1949.

Kaston, B. J. *Spiders of Connecticut.* Bulletin of the Connecticut Geological Natural History Survey, 70, 1948. (Centered on Connecticut, but highly useful reference for spiders of the eastern United States.)

Levi, Herbert W. *A Guide to Spiders.* Golden Press, 1968.

Shuttlesworth, D. E. *The Story of Spiders.* Garden City Books, Doubleday, 1959. (Lively, accurate children's book.)

Crickets

Pierce, George W. *The Songs of Insects.* Harvard, 1949.

Teale, Edwin Way. *The Strange Lives of Familiar Insects.* Dodd, Mead, 1962. (Offbeat observations plus loads of information on a variety of insects.)

Earthworms

Darwin, Charles. *The Formation of the Vegetable Mould.* Appleton & Co., 1882. (Amazingly thorough and accurate after almost a century.)

Roots, B. L. *New Biology No. 21: Famous Animals: The Earthworm.* Penguin, 1956.

Social Insects

Crompton, John. *Ways of the Ant.* Houghton Mifflin, 1954.

Goetsch, Wilhelm. *The Ants.* University of Michigan Press, 1957.

Maeterlinck, M. *The Life of the White Ant.* Dodd, Mead, 1939.

Michener, C. D. and M. H. *American Social Insects.* Van Nostrand, 1951.
Peckham, G. W. and E. G. *Wasps, Social and Solitary.* Houghton Mifflin, 1905.
Plath, Otto. *Bumblebees and Their Ways.* Macmillan, 1934.
Snyder, Thomas. *Our Enemy the Termite.* Comstock, 1948.

Biological Catalogs

Turtox Biological Supplies Catalog; General Biologicals, Inc., 8200 South Hoyne Avenue, Chicago, Ill. 60620
Ward's Catalog for Biology and the Earth Sciences; Ward's Natural Science Establishment, Inc., P.O. Box 1712, Rochester, N.Y. 14603

Index

About the Author

Robert Gannon lives in Tillson, New York, but has a 19-acre farm in nearby High Falls. It is there he found the rock he writes about. This is his second book about nature. The first, written with John Walsh and published by Dutton, was *Time Is Short and the Water Rises,* which required research in the tropical rain forest of Surinam, South America. When not traveling, Mr. Gannon is usually writing magazine articles and over 150 of them have been published in such magazines as *Reader's Digest, Saturday Evening Post,* and *True.* He also writes the column "Pet Pointers" in *Family Circle* and is the Adventure Editor of *Popular Science.*

About the Artist

Stefan Martin spent many hours in the garden of his home in Roosevelt, New Jersey, sketching rocks and then turning them over to examine the ground beneath. He suspects his puzzled neighbors began to worry about him. Mr. Martin has done many technical drawings for magazines such as *Scientific American,* but for *What's Under a Rock?* he wanted to produce illustrations that were first of all artwork, although accurate in technical details. He used pen and ink for the finished drawings and at times spattered ink from a toothbrush to give the effect of soil. Mr. Martin is also well known for his handsome wood engravings that have appeared in several children's books, including *Small Pond* by Marguerite Walters, also published by Dutton.

The text of this book is set in Caledonia and the titles are set in Deepdene Italic. The book is printed by offset.